EXPLORING BRITAIN'S COUNTRY GARDENS

AA

Editor
Donna Wood

Designer
Tracey Butler

Picture Researcher
Alice Earle

Image retouching and internal repro
Sarah Montgomery

*Cartography provided by the Mapping Services
Department of AA Publishing*

Contains Ordnance Survey data © Crown copyright
and database right 2012

Production
Lorraine Taylor

Produced by AA Publishing

Published by AA Publishing (a trading name of
AA Media Limited, whose registered office is
Fanum House, Basing View, Basingstoke RG21 4EA;
registered number 06112600).

A04753

The contents of this book are believed correct at
the time of printing. Nevertheless, the publishers
cannot be held responsible for any errors or
omissions or for changes in the details given in this
book or for the consequences of any reliance on
the information provided by the same. This does
not affect your statutory rights.

Printed in China by C&C Offset Printing Co. Ltd

theAA.com/shop

OPENING TIMES

We give a general guide to opening times in
this book, but please be aware that this refers
to the gardens only, not the attached premises,
which may or may not open to the public at
different times. Many gardens reserve the right
to change their opening times without warning.
We strongly advise that you telephone and/or
consult the garden's website before travelling.

Right: Astilbes by the ponds at Hodnet Hall gardens

EXPLORING BRITAIN'S
COUNTRY GARDENS

LOCATOR MAP

SCOTLAND &
THE BORDERS

NORTHERN
ENGLAND

WALES &
THE MARCHES

CENTRAL ENGLAND
& EAST ANGLIA

SOUTH WEST
ENGLAND

SOUTH & SOUTH EAST
ENGLAND

CONTENTS

INTRODUCTION

by Pamela Westland

Exploring Britain's Country Gardens: the title has an implied invitation that is, surely, irresistible to any garden-lover, the opportunity to marvel at the skill and ingenuity, learn from the expertise and share the passion of dedicated gardeners from coast to coast. Here is a selection of gardens with, collectively, a wealth of interest and excitement to offer both the casual viewer and the practised garden visitor. Some of the gardens are well-known and visited by thousands of enthusiasts every year, and others, enticingly, are yet to be discovered on that scale. It is hoped that this book will encourage you both to renew your acquaintance with your own favourites and to visit others for the first time.

Every one of the gardens is a rich source of inspiration and has at least one facet that any gardener could adapt on any scale, and many are a source of encouragement and even courage. It has been immensely exciting to discover the determination of some gardeners to overcome the disadvantages of inhospitable terrain, a seemingly unworkable site or an unfriendly climate. There are many examples of gardens created by people who refuse to take 'can't' for an answer and have created a more favourable micro-climate, defeated notoriously punishing gales, salt spray or relentless drought and created gardens that have an other-worldly quality. The message is that if you yearn to create an idyllic haven on a windswept hillside, go for it!

The awareness of climate change and its continuing effects on the environment has caused many gardeners to rethink what is appropriate and sustainable to grow in their own space. Garden design, even classical styles, has always evolved over time, largely through fashion and personal preference. But now there are greater forces to consider. Many garden owners are replanting existing borders with more drought-tolerant plants, an exciting challenge that many of us might care to take up. As water becomes an ever more precious commodity in many parts of the world, it is the judicious and responsible reuse of minimal amounts, be it in cascades or rills, pools or fountains, that has that therapeutic, satisfying, sought-after effect.

Visitors who thrill to walking in the footsteps of history or literature will find plenty to interest them. If you fancy wandering round a rose walk where King Henry VIII might have strolled with his bride Catherine Howard, or pausing beneath the oak tree that was a favourite resting place of Queen Elizabeth I when her court was in residence, then go to Chenies Manor. Such an experience would surely bring history to life for many a schoolchild. Or visit Hodsock Priory, another property favoured

Below: Paths once trodden by royalty at Chenies Manor

Right: Wire sculpture by Derek Kinzett in the walled rose garden at Newstead Abbey

by royalty. Henry VIII stayed there, too, as did three other monarchs, Henry II, John and Edward I.

Literature had an important role to play at Newstead Abbey, where one can see admittedly just the remains of the oak which ten-year-old Lord Byron planted in the garden on succeeding to the title; you could add meaning to your visit by reading the poem he wrote, movingly, on leaving the property. Woodchippings, too, has a literary connection: might Flora Thompson have walked through that very woodland in Juniper Hill when seeking inspiration for *Lark Rise to Candleford*, the rural classic she set there?

History lives on in many of the gardens through plants that were discovered and brought back by the great Victorian plant hunters. Some wealthy landowners sponsored major expeditions; Borde Hill, for example, became (and still is) a showplace for rare and unusual species discovered on expeditions to faraway places. The magnificent magnolias at Caerhays Castle owe their origins to the then owner's sponsorship of two plant collectors, George Forrest and E H Wilson, and the glorious rhododendrons at Crarae Garden have their roots in a family member's plant-collecting excursions to the Chinese province of Kansu and to Burma.

Lawrence Johnston, who created the magnificent gardens at Hidcote Manor, both sponsored and took part in plant-hunting expeditions that resulted in the cultivation of over 40 new species. Here at Hidcote Johnston designed what he called 'a garden of rooms', each one concealed behind high hedges of holly, beech, hornbeam or yew, and each with a different planting scheme; a concept so widely followed today as to seem almost commonplace. This idea of creating 'hidden' spaces, of leading the visitor from one enclosed area to another, allows designers to be bolder than they might care to be over a larger span. The more a garden is subdivided, the more opportunity there is to experiment on a small scale. Be prepared for another wow factor round the next corner!

The influence of a few iconic gardeners, Johnston among them, is evident not only in many of our featured gardens but in our own, too. Gardeners everywhere who plant deep herbaceous borders for stunning visual effect – with, perhaps, hot reds, purples and oranges reaching a fiery crescendo at the centre – are forever in the debt of Gertrude Jekyll, artist turned garden designer. See for yourself the sheer beauty of her artistry at the Manor House at Upton Grey where the gardens she created have now been faithfully restored according to her own plans; at Loseley Park where, while taking afternoon tea, she drew up plans for a herbaceous border with her signature cool-hot-cool scheme, choosing as she always did plants not only for colour but

for texture, shape and perfume too; or visit Hestercombe House where Jekyll planted the Grey Walk.

The mixing and mingling of everyday plants with rarer species and the painting of colourful tapestries of ground-cover plants are legacies left to gardeners everywhere by Margery Fish, another passionate plantswoman-cum-designer. You can walk in her footsteps at East Lambrook Manor, the garden she created for herself, and see her influence in countless other gardens we feature.

Another constant theme is the varied and imaginative use of evergreen hedges. These are used not only to form compartments but to enhance perspective, frame and 'borrow' views. On an even more practical level they can act as windshields to protect more tender plants; not only evergreen hedges but topiary structures too. From the magnificent, centuries-old flights of fancy designed by French gardener Guillaume Beaumont at Levens Hall to the balls, cones, domes, pyramids, cubes, helter-skelters or random shapes deployed in other gardens, topiary forms are an important element of garden design: horticultural statuary. Whether they are grown in rows with almost military precision, are encroached upon – embraced, even – by rambling plants, or upstaged by unrestrained neighbouring planting, these elements can set the tone of a garden, adding formality where it is wanted or detracting from it where it is not.

Looking around a garden it is always fascinating to know what – apart from the clear influence of iconic designers – led gardeners along a particular design path. Inspiration, you will find, comes from the most unexpected sources. Here are designs of gardens, or areas within them, inspired by Persian carpets (Attadale); Elizabethan embroideries known as 'fancy work' (the Fancy Garden at Herterton House); the dining-room ceiling, carried out in the planting of herbs at Mannington Hall; a hunting scene clipped out in a yew hedge at Knightshayes Court gardens; and even the Glamorganshire cockle-fishing industry carried out in shell-shaped topiary at Ridler's Garden.

Many of the featured gardens have been shaped by the deeply contrasting influences of Italian Renaissance art and Japanese culture. Marvel at the formal landscaping, geometric formations and classical statuary so artistically set out by architect-turned-landscape gardener Harold Peto at Iford Manor. His influence is evidenced in several gardens we describe, but this is the one he designed for himself. As proof positive that scale is not of paramount importance, see the pleasing formality that can be achieved by the skilful deployment of geometry and placement in the comparatively modest Raworth Garden. And to illustrate that the simplicity of Japanese garden design can live in good neighbourliness with traditional country-garden profusion, turn, as just one example, to the pages describing Haddon Lake House, where there is a Japanese-style courtyard, mixed fruit and flower beds and vibrant borders in near-primary colours.

Many of the gardeners whose work is featured here are passionate not just about plants in general but about one or more species in particular, and some make a significant contribution to the breeding of those species. Here, often, is a chance for the visitor to learn first-hand what it takes in terms of aspect, soil and dedication to grow such plants to the highest standard. From tulips planted in artistic drifts at Chenies Manor; hellebores at Woodchippings; salvias at Great Comp; arisaema and clematis at Creux Baillot Cottage; to the blue and mauve bearded irises that form such a spectacular tapestry of colour in the Elizabethan knot garden at Doddington Hall, these are opportunities not to be missed.

It is the proud assertion of the Jersey Island gardener that she has at least one of her treasured 200 clematis plants in flower on every day of the year: no mean achievement. This ambition, to provide year-round interest, is shared by many garden owners who strive to extend the time when they can welcome and inspire visitors. Even so, there might be 'best time to view' dates on their websites, so always check before planning a visit. For gardens that specialise in romantic beds and borders – pergolas too – of roses and peonies, and there are many, June and early July are the not-to-be-missed dates. In other gardens borders that might have near-year-round interest become hotbeds of colour in August and September – think penstemons, phlox, Oriental poppies, dahlias, gladioli and salvias. And later in the season gardens known for their range of ornamental grasses, leaf colour and late-flowering shrubs make an autumn visit an uplifting experience.

Moving on to winter, visitors – suitably clad – can enjoy gardens in completely different moods. 'Think leaf, bark and berries' advise the two innovative gardeners at East Ruston Old Vicarage and, practising what they preach, they invite visitors to appreciate the many variegated leaf forms of holly and other evergreens, the from-white-to-rusty-red stems of birches, the textural trunks of eucalyptus, the brilliant hues of dogwood stems and the bold reds, yellows and oranges of holly and other berries.

Just when it seems that winter will never finish and – no matter how dramatic the displays of bark and berries – garden-lovers long for spring, there is good news. More and more gardens, many of which we feature, are specialising in massed displays of spring bulbs and bringing back that much-loved country tradition, Snowdrop Sunday, when some – not all – serve warming soup and snacks. There are snowdrop trails that lead, variously, through woodland, over bridges, across streams, past a Norman keep, around a lake, along an ancient moat and, hopefully, back for a mug of steaming soup. As you wander past carpets of snowdrops that number, at Hodsock Priory, millions of these sparkling white flowers and thrill to the brilliance of myriad tiny naturalised daffodils, crocus and cyclamen your heart lifts: you know that the garden-visiting season has started all over again.

What incredible diversity! Just as some gardeners have designed enclosed micro-gardens with a variety of themes, others have created oases with the look and even the ambience of faraway places. Yet others have sought to design gardens that are at one with the environment and, running wild on the boundaries, seem to merge with the landscape beyond. As you will find throughout the book, where the imagination of gardeners is concerned, there are no boundaries.

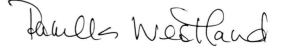

③

SOUTH WEST ENGLAND | 1

England's south west, with its dwindling peninsula pointing out into the Atlantic, gives a stronger sense of Island Britain than anywhere else in the country. Defined by its rugged coastline, its picture-book villages and its bustling country towns, the region attracts those who long to escape the stresses of urban Britain. Here, in the glorious south west, you will find gardens constructed at the heart of exquisite Cotswold villages, others created on the fertile banks of rivers and trout streams, even a garden situated far out in the Atlantic Ocean and warmed by the Gulf Stream. A Devonian garden, its foundations laid entirely with local materials, is so perfectly at one with its surroundings that it might 'just have happened'. It did not, of course – it's the result of endless thought and care – but the same 'natural' impression is given by many other glorious gardens that sit so comfortably in a region favoured by a benign climate.

BARNSLEY HOUSE

4 miles (6.5km) north east of Cirencester | Usually open daily; contact first | Tel: 01285 740000 | www.barnsleyhouse.com

Barnsley is surely one of the prettiest stone villages in the Cotswolds and there, in perfect harmony and keeping its charms hidden until the last moment, stands Barnsley House. Once the abrupt entrance drive has been negotiated, the immediate and lasting impression is one of harmony. The honey-coloured Queen Anne house stands serenely amid 4 acres (1.6ha) of intimate garden enclosures interrupted by a sweeping lawn with softly coloured herbaceous borders.

Rosemary Verey and her late husband, David, began to design the garden in the 1960s, and although the notion of natural growth is strongly evident, the bones of the garden are strong and maintenance is at a high level. On an axis from the drawing-room door a stone path, with its texture deliberately softened by clumps of geraniums and rock roses, runs straight to the centre of the south lawn, which is flanked by generous plantings of aquilegias, stachys, phlomis and

others in soft, muted colours. Beyond this, mature trees, including a purple sycamore, an atlas cedar and a silver-grey white poplar, provide a marvellous contrast of foliage colours, textures and shapes.

Near to the house on the western side is a delightful knot garden, its little box hedges set amid gravel in the manner of the formal parterres so popular in the 16th and 17th centuries. The two squares of the knot have different designs.

In the 1960s David Verey moved a temple from Fairford Park to the south-east corner of the garden, thus creating a peaceful vista leading the eye over the richly covered lily pond, through two iron gates flanked by statuesque cypresses, to a charming wall fountain beyond.

Alongside Mrs Verey's potager, or decorative kitchen garden, runs a wonderful laburnum tunnel which in spring is thickly covered with yellow panicles reaching down to meet the tall, mauve alliums that rise from beneath its shade.

The potager, inspired by the one at the Chateau de Villandry in the Loire valley, and by *The Country Housewife's Garden* written in 1617 by William Lawson, is a truly remarkable creation. Brick paths in many different patterns criss-cross the area; the beds themselves are planted with red and green varieties of lettuce and other vegetables, while sweet peas grow close to gooseberries and onions, cabbages, lavender and strawberries.

In perfect harmony with the stone wall behind them, and indeed with the profusion and variety of the planting throughout the beds and borders, two stone statues of country girls holding baskets generously filled with flowers flank the gateway to the potager beyond. It may be observed that the layout of the potager is typical of Barnsley House garden as a whole – a charming mixture of nonchalance and formality.

Left: The honey-coloured Queen Anne-style Barnsley House is set in 4 acres (1.6ha) of lovely gardens

Top right: The softly lit temple in the garden's south-east corner is the ideal spot for an alfresco meal on a summer's evening

Right: In the former garden of Rosemary Verey, *Allium hollandicum* 'Purple Sensation' is planted to optimum effect inside the shady laburnum tunnel

CAERHAYS CASTLE Cornwall PL26 6LY

9 miles (15km) south west of Austell | Open daily mid-Feb to early Jun | Tel: 01872 501310 | **www.caerhays.co.uk**

On the south coast of Cornwall, close to the River Luney which reaches the sea in Porthluney Cove, is the vast and romantic Caerhays Castle. Built in the early years of the 19th century in the Gothic style by John Nash for John Bettesworth Trevanion, Caerhays came into the hands of the Williams family in 1853. It was John Charles Williams who created the gardens and financially supported the great plant hunters, E H Wilson and George Forrest. Today, still owned by the same family, Caerhays has an unrivalled collection of magnolias and shrubs which derive from the enterprise.

J C Williams also specialised in the cultivation of daffodils, under the expert guidance of the Reverend Engelheart.

Leaving the west side of the castle you approach the Auklandii Gardens where, on the right, there are some great *Rhododendron arboreum* hybrids which are more than a century old, as well as an oak which was probably sent to Caerhays from Louisiana by the great plant collector, Professor Sargent. Beyond the terrace, with its views of the house and the beach, the main path leads into the Tin Garden past some spectacular magnolias. The biggest

of these is the *Magnolia veitchii* 'Peter Veitch', which came from Veitch's great nursery in 1920, and a *Magnolia campbellii*, introduced to Britain in 1865. Rather curiously, its flowers appear before the leaves. Unfortunately the big storm of 1990 uprooted two large magnolias, each 80 feet (24.3 metres) high. In this part of the garden there are both a fine rhododendron hybrid 'Crossbill' and a *Camellia reticulata* 'Captain Rawes', which is almost a century old.

To the right of the main route is Mr Roger's Quarry, where you can admire the best variety of *Magnolia campbellii* at Caerhays, *mollicomata* 'Lanarth', which produces cyclamen-purple flowers. In addition to his work with rhododendrons, J C Williams crossed two species of camellia, producing the *Camellia williamsii* hybrids which are seen extensively throughout the country today. A clump of one of the best varieties, 'J C Williams', which has single pink flowers in the late spring, is to be seen in the quarry.

Above the main path is a screen of laurel, a striking *Rhododendron sinogrande* and two hybrids raised at Caerhays, 'Emma Williams' and 'Veryan Bay'. The latter was one of the last hybrids cultivated by Williams. The steep path down from the Donkey Shoe past the Old Quarry to the castle gives a splendid view of one of the largest hybrid camellias in the garden, 'November Pink', as well as azaleas and *Styrax japonica*, which produces white, bell-shaped flowers in early summer.

Cornwall is a county rich in glorious gardens and Caerhays is without doubt one of the most remarkable.

Left: The castle viewed through *Magnolia dawsoniana* located off the path to the Rookery Gate

Right: A springtime view of the garden with several different magnolias visible

Below: *Magnolia* 'Pickards Sundew'

6 miles (9.5km) south west of Pewsey | Open selected days by appointment | Tel: 07810 483984

South west of the Wiltshire town of Pewsey, the River Avon flows between the east and west Salisbury Plain. On the east bank stands Chisenbury Priory, a red-brick Jacobean house with a Georgian façade, set in charming gardens of about 5 acres (2ha), created during the past 35 years by the owners, Mr and Mrs Alastair Robb.

In front of the house two borders frame the entrance. These were designed by Tom Stuart-Smith and planted in 2008. The fluffy-leaved thalictrum, the evergreen perennial veronicastrum with its delicate pink flowers, echinacea (coneflower) and *Penstemon* 'Raven' create a pink/purple theme, interspersed by grasses including *Stipa gigantea* and *S. calamagrostis*. The walls are covered by a profusion of roses and clematis. Behind the house a striking galvanised steel pergola leads down to the lower lawn under a canopy of roses.

A flight of wide steps runs through a border which separates the upper lawn from the lower one, which has a leat running at the bottom. This area is planted with hostas, ligularia, astilbes, *Rheum palmatum* and gunnera. Specimen trees and some interesting shrubs, including a fine *Cornus kousa chinensis*, and *Staphylea colchica* and *S. holocarpa* surround the lawn.

Beyond the wall, the character of the gardens undergoes another change, with an extensive wildflower meadow and, against the wall, another cottage border, dominated by hollyhocks underplanted with geraniums. Above that is a parterre, a white garden and a walled area with a circular pond.

Left: A wooden bench occupies a shady corner under the steel pergola

Top right: The large apple sculpture doubles as a seat

Right: A graceful water feature in the lily-filled pond

There are many rare South African plants at Chisenbury, the most tender of which are grown in containers and moved into the greenhouse during the winter.

Many of the plant species that the visitor will have admired during a tour of the garden are propagated here and are for sale, as is a light, white wine made from the Chisenbury vines. There is much to admire in this beautiful garden which, by its diversity of habitat and charming planting, leaves the visitor both uplifted and inspired.

THE COURTS GARDEN Wiltshire BA14 6RR

The beautiful gardens of The Courts, now owned by the National Trust, retain a sense of mystery, standing as they do behind high stone walls in the centre of the village of Holt. It was once thought that The Courts was so named because it was to this building that the cloth weavers of Bradford-on-Avon, a mile away, brought their disputes for settlement; it is, however, certain that at one time cloth was made on the site in a cloth mill that stood next to the house.

When in 1900 the well-known architect Sir George Hastings bought The Courts, he introduced many of the architectural features to its garden – including the yew and box hedges as a background for the decorative stone ornaments and the ring of stone pillars, themselves decorative 'climbing frames' for roses; he also built the conservatory. From 1921 it was owned by Major T C E Goff and Lady Cecilie, his wife, and it was she who, influenced by Gertrude Jekyll, laid out the series of 'garden rooms' at The Courts which offer an ever-changing series of vistas and make the visitor feel that the gardens are even larger than their 7 acres (2.8ha).

The garden is reached through an avenue of pleached limes at the front of the house. To the east of the house is a lawn dominated by eight stone pillars, while the left-hand border is planted with penstemons, geraniums, irises, violas and

Centaurea hypoleuca 'John Coutts'. Opposite is a mainly herbaceous border bright with montbretia and berberis, while the bedding plants are modern cultivars of the annual rudbeckias.

The lily pond was made by Lady Cecilie Goff, and its paved area is dominated in autumn by sumach and a purple berberis underplanted with bergenias and diascias. The pond itself boasts dark-red, pink and white waterlilies, and is surrounded by the pink-flowered *Dierama pulcherrimum* (angel's fishing rod) and *Iris sibirica* (Siberian flag). The borders beyond the lily pond are filled with hostas, astilbes, rodgersias, and a fragrant *Viburnum carlesii*.

A path runs around the natural shape of the lower pond to re-emerge in front of a stone pavilion where there are two deep flower borders planted with pink, yellow and purple-flowering perennials, including many hemerocallis. The Venetian Gate borders, which lead on to the house lawn, are edged with lilies, red hot pokers, lychnis and echinops.

At the corner of the main lawn, over to the west, are the remains of an African seat, once covered with a grass roof, while a path behind it is edged with clumps of Japanese sacred bamboo and angel's fishing rod.

At the end of the main lawn, the sundial is surrounded by artemisias, flag irises and two clipped, weeping pears, while the blue and yellow borders are rich with geraniums, euphorbias, achilleas and Michaelmas daisies.

Left: The Yew Walk features a display of cone-shaped yews on one side and plantings on the other, including red hot pokers (kniphofia)

Below: The lily-covered Dye Pool is surrounded by colour and topiary

EAST LAMBROOK MANOR Somerset TA13 5HH

 1½ miles (3km) north east of South Petherton | **Open selected days Feb to Oct** | **Tel: 01460 240328** | **www.eastlambrook.co.uk**

There are many gardens in Britain and beyond that owe their inspiration to the innovative planting ideas of the late Margery Fish, gardening writer and passionate plantswoman. Think of the borders where old-fashioned plants mingle and sometimes intertwine with contemporary ones; where everyday plants complement rarer species; where ground-cover plants paint a low-level tapestry of colour and texture. These and many other ideas, so readily accepted now, were the hallmark of Margery Fish's romantic style of gardening.

She and her husband Walter bought the East Lambrook property, a small 15th-century manor house and a run-down former chicken farm, in 1938. At the time Mrs Fish had little or no gardening expertise but she soon became almost obsessive about it, putting her ideas into practice and, she has said, making her own mistakes along the way. For the next three decades, until her death in 1969, Margery Fish created one of the most iconic cottage gardens of that century; one which is a lasting legacy to her skill and zeal. After her death the garden passed to

her nephew and now, several owners later, is under the care and stewardship of Gail and Mike Werkmeister, who bought the property in 2008. As a fitting tribute to its creator, the garden was granted Grade I status by English Heritage in 1992.

On entering the garden via the main gate you pass first through the gravelled barton (former farmyard) with its mulberry planted in 1969; above this, in the centre of the garden, is the recently restored 17th-century Malthouse with café and small gallery. To the left is the main lawn with

Left: Clumps of snowdrops on the banks of the Ditch

Above: *Betula utilis jacquemontii* with *Polemonium* 'Lambrook Mauve' beneath

Right: *Geranium malviflorum*

Below right: Cool-water shades of blue and green

many fine trees, including the *Acer pseudoplatanus* 'Leopoldii' which Margery Fish so admired when she first saw the house. Beyond this, crooked stone paths wend their way through Mrs Fish's famous terraces, principally planted with perennials including many unusual varieties, and the Silver Garden, with its collection of Mediterranean-style silver-leaved plants including *Artemisia* 'Lambrook Silver', a cultivar selected by her.

These areas are separated by low clipped hedges of *Lonicera nitida,* which also surround the lawn above.

21

Moving on via the top lawn to the back of the Malthouse brings you to the Lido, a damp area full of shade- and moisture-loving plants including many primulas, with a magnificent white wisteria as a backdrop. Beyond it is the area known as the Ditch and, to the right, the new Woodland Garden which was completely replanted in 2005 by the head gardener, Mark Stainer, who has worked at East Lambrook Manor since 1975. This is home to a breathtaking display of rare and unusual snowdrops in late January and early February. As spring advances these are replaced by the blue of scillas and bluebells and many

shades of cream, white, pink and purple from an extensive collection of hellebores (mainly *Helleborus orientalis*).

A vast collection of unusual small bulbs and herbaceous plants give a succession of interest throughout the year with many delightful plant combinations. *Polemonium* 'Lambrook Mauve' (Jacob's ladder) looks particularly attractive in May next to the white stems of *Betula utilis* var. *jacquemontii*. Perhaps it is the summer flowering, an ever-changing kaleidoscope of subtle colour, that most typifies the influence of the garden's creator. There are many old roses, some

clambering up fruit trees; the tall, stately stems of *Nectaroscordum siculum* with their clusters of white bell-shaped flowers; geraniums, for which the garden is famous, mingling with aquilegia and *Gladiolus byzantinus* pushing their crimson-red spires through euphorbia – a truly glorious sight.

Beyond the Woodland Garden the gravel path returns you to the barton via the Sundial Garden and the Green Garden, currently being restored after having been 'lost' under a sea of vinca for over 30 years.

Colour retains its vibrancy as summer gives way to autumn, when the fiery hues of the trees and late-flowering perennials including aster, kniphofia and rudbeckia put the seeding heads of tall grasses such as cortaderia and miscanthus metaphorically in the shade.

Margery Fish took great pleasure in sharing her plants with visitors and was generous with her gifts. Gradually this policy of 'spreading the word' through the distribution of species and unusual plants developed into a business, and today in the Margery Fish Plant Nursery visitors can buy many of her favourite plants, some of which she introduced herself.

In this way, not only her influence but plant species she admired so much and used so imaginatively, live on in cottage-style gardens far and wide.

Left: The Silver Garden in July

Above: The beautiful blush pink and crimson blooms of *Rosa gallica* 'Versicolor', popularly known as *Rosa mundi*

Right: White wisteria falls like snow from a high wall

FORDE ABBEY GARDENS Somerset TA20 4LU

4 miles (6.5km) south east of Chard | Open daily | Tel: 01460 221290 | **www.fordeabbey.co.uk**

During a moment of quiet reflection, perhaps spent beside the Great Pond which once powered the monastery grain mill, one might call to mind the work of the Cistercian monks who supported themselves by tending this land around the 12th-century monastic building. In the intervening centuries the gardens have several times fallen into disrepair and consequently have undergone several major redevelopments and refurbishments, but the legacy of tranquillity and sense of calm remain.

The principal landscaping was set out in the early 18th century when the property was owned by Sir Francis Gwyn and, it is thought, he called on Guillaume Beaumont, a pupil of André Le Nôtre, to assist with the layout. Strong elements of this design

remain – the extensive lawns, the giant yews, the walls, the cascades and three lower pools that augment the original monastic one, now home to a devoted pair of swans. A change of ownership in the mid-19th century saw the creation of a typically Victorian garden with dense shrubberies and an over-emphasis on dark foliage and flowers.

In 2005 Mark and Lisa Roper, parents of Alice Kennard, the present owner, celebrated their family's 100 years at Forde Abbey with the installation of the Centenary Fountain in the Mermaid Pond. With a 160-foot (48.7-metre) flow, this is the highest powered fountain in England. The Long Pond has its focal point, too. At its head there is the Ionic Tempietto, a small circular temple capped

by an intricate wrought iron dome that casts intriguing reflections.

A bog garden created in the early 1900s is presided over by the structural forms of giant gunnera, royal ferns and hostas. In spring tall white and yellow glossy spathes of lysichiton precede the large fresh green leaves of plants that can reach 3 feet (1 metre) in height, and colour is reinforced by irises, meconopsis and waterside-loving forms of lobelia.

In other parts of the gardens spring is heralded in spectacular ways. At a time when the front of the house is cloaked in pale mauve wisteria, thick borders of wallflowers seem to spray the air with their perfume, and carpets of Dutch crocus (*Crocus vernus*) cover 10 acres (4ha) of lawns. In order to ensure their continuity, the plants are left to die down in the long grass which is not cut until the end of June. A woodland spring garden structured with camellias, magnolias, azaleas and rhododendrons has a confetti-like spattering of dog's-tooth violets (*Erythronium dens-canis*) with their pretty pink, purple and white flowers and mottled leaves.

The herbaceous borders which are reflected in the long canal become an explosion of colour from midsummer onwards when dahlias, asters, delphiniums and aconitums combine to create a floral tapestry, whilst in the facing border, protected by a high wall, there are carpenteria, lace-cap hydrangeas and the yellow-flowering evergreen shrubs, azaras.

The Beech House, planted with saplings of pleached willow in the 1930s as a hide for bird-watching, is now seen as a delightful, living folly, one that is complete with a roof and small windows: an alternative version of a tree house. Trees have a significant role at Forde Abbey. Geoffrey Roper, grandfather of the present owner, planted an arboretum and increased other areas of woodland in the 1940s. The Mount is dominated by giant redwoods, incense cedars (*Calocedrus decurrens*) and Oriental plane trees. Large Douglas firs (*Pseudotsuga menziesii*) are a legacy from the previous owners.

The walled kitchen garden, restored in the 19th century with extensive greenhouses and now producing an abundance of fruit, vegetables and flowers for cutting, is perhaps the closest link with the gardens as they were in their monastic period, over 800 years ago.

THE GARDEN HOUSE Devon PL20 7LQ

1½ miles (3km) west of Yelverton | Usually open daily Mar to Oct | Tel: 01822 854769 | **www.thegardenhouse.org.uk**

A walled garden created around the ruins of a 16th-century vicarage; a rugged stone structure of snaking paths and overgrown walls; a wildflower meadow that merges seamlessly into the moorland scenery beyond; a from-gold-to-russet acer glade; a 'magic' stone circle on a grassy knoll; and, everywhere, skilful and inspirational planting: it is tempting to say that this Devonshire garden has everything.

At its heart is the 2-acre (0.8ha) walled garden created in 1947 by Lionel Fortescue, an Eton schoolmaster and avid plant collector who lived at The Garden House with his wife Katharine from the 1940s until

his death in 1981. The wow factor is not accidental. Enter the enclosed garden and it is as if the lights have been switched on in a room. Cascades of wisteria, colourful clusters of rare shrubs – mahonia, azaleas and rhododendrons – and species of herbaceous plants are woven around the ruins of the imposing granite tower and thatched stone kitchen that were part of the vicarage.

The four terraces in the walled garden are linked by narrow flights of steps and ramps made with local stone, the natural materials – featured elsewhere in the garden in walls and follies – forming an important link with the countryside beyond. Fortescue's chosen

successor at The Garden House, Keith Wiley, and the current head gardener Matt Bishop have maintained his practice of using only the best plants and arranging them in a naturalistic way.

This principle, now carried out by three successive gardeners, creates the impression that the garden has just happened. Cushions of purple asters and orange-peel heleniums, bronze achillea, citrus-yellow helianthus and clusters of flame-red canna are punctuated by billowy plumes of miscanthus. The planting is skilful and yet it appears random. In a similar way the hollyhock-like flowers of sidalcea, feathery, frondy astilbes in red,

pink and mauve, brilliant scarlet spires of penstemon and clusters of more orange, blue and yellow flowers mingle and merge like colours on an artist's palette. Seeds scatter and are allowed to thrive as they would in the wild, and the impression is delightful.

If the walled garden were the only area open to visitors – and thankfully it is not – that alone would be worth the journey. Beyond its walls the garden adopts a number of different characteristics. The South African garden, originally inspired by Keith Wiley's travels, was replanted in 2004 by Matt Bishop. The drama of the planting is enhanced by a range of shaped, slightly elevated beds representing an undulating landscape. Here there are drifts of the daisy-like flower heads of arctotis in colours ranging from orange and yellow to purple and red; several prolific varieties of osteospermum – daisy shapes again; and, in pretty profusion, the golden-orange eschscholzia – all linked together with clusters of evergreen grasses from New Zealand. It is a brilliant kaleidoscope of sun-bright colours.

A round, thatched summer house on a high bank is the focal point of one of Wiley's innovations, known as the Ovals. It is a sculpture in stone, with dry stone walls and narrow paths zigzagging down to an enveloping oval brick path. The planting is special. Large clumps of glossy green-leaved hostas intermingle with light, bright green ferns, swathes of cream astilbes and a single clump of red salvias. That is the background to a casual spattering of yellow Welsh poppies. If an artist had flicked yellow paint randomly and generously onto a largely green canvas it would have looked like that.

On a north-facing slope brought under cultivation only in 1993 the Acer Glade vibrates with colour at different levels throughout the year. In March at ground level it is bejewelled with thousands of crocus.

Left: Plants merge like colours on an artist's palette

Above: Sloping terraces and narrow paths zigzag away from the Ovals

In April and May attention is focused at a higher level as Lionel Fortescue's spectacular azaleas and rhododendrons paint the glade pink, red and purple. And then in October the area is a breathtaking harmony of the red and russet, bronze and yellow foliage of Japanese maples with – as if that were not enough – misty views of the South Devon countryside with Buckland Monachorum parish church at its heart. An avenue of limes linking the garden and the church is a reminder that this was, at one time, the vicarage garden.

The mood changes in the nostalgic cottage garden where foxgloves, poppies and eschscholzia harmonise; in the quarry garden shimmering with alpines; around the front lawn area where in winter there are now popular snowdrop walks; and in a flowery, colour-splashed meadow which might just have sprung up unaided and untamed from the rocky Dartmoor soil. The 'magic circle', a ring of fallen stones encircling a quartet of irregular-sized monoliths on a grassy knoll, might perhaps have pervaded this land with its mystical aura for centuries. One thing is certain. The whole of this inspirational and innovative garden has a supremely magical quality.

The son of a painter, Lionel Fortescue was notoriously exacting not only in his choice of plants – nothing but the very best was good enough – but in their precise colour. It is said that he once tore up large clumps of Himalayan poppies (*Meconopsis betonicifolia*) – not the easiest plants in the world to grow – because they had turned out to be the wrong shade of blue.

HEALE GARDENS Wiltshire SP4 6NT

4 miles (6.5km) north of Salisbury | Open selected days Feb to Sep | Tel: 01722 782504 | www.healegarden.co.uk

Ask four garden-lovers to nominate their favourite season to visit Heale House garden and you might easily receive four different and equally valid replies. Open to visitors for eight months of the year, the garden does not have a between-seasons period when one exuberant explosion of flowering is over and the next is yet to come – it has an ever-changing kaleidoscope of colour.

The garden is situated on the banks of the River Avon and has the added advantages of tributaries of the river meandering through it, with sparkling trout streams and quiet backwaters creating perfect conditions for shade-loving species and colourful cascades of trailing plants. It is in part an architectural garden, in part a plantsman's garden, but a productive one, too. The working kitchen garden blends a formal layout – a beautiful potager – with wide, densely fruitful tunnels of apples and pears. One of these, particularly delightful in spring when the fruit trees are in blossom, is underplanted with white tulips and silver-leaved plants.

The red brick house built by Sir William Greene in the late 16th century took its place in the history books when King Charles II took refuge there for several nights in October 1651 before fleeing to France; the king later reported his experience to the diarist Samuel Pepys. After several changes of ownership, the property was bought in 1894 by the Honourable Louis Greville, great-uncle of the present owner, Guy Rasch. The foundations of the garden were laid shortly afterwards when Greville commissioned the architect and gardener Harold Peto, and many of the early 20th-century structural features and formal plantings remain.

Left: The thatched teahouse. Overhung by weeping willow and approached by the scarlet Nikko bridge (right), these Japanese treasures were shipped back from Tokyo by the British diplomat Louis Greville

A large lawn to the south leads to the trout stream and, where it divides, to Louis Greville's Japanese garden, situated on an island. Greville brought back the thatched teahouse and the brilliant scarlet Nikko bridge when he left the British Embassy in Tokyo, where he was a diplomat. Overhung by weeping willows and close to light-dappled woodland, it is a delightful feature.

Carpets of spring bulbs colour-wash the woodlands and meadows along the river banks. Early in February, parts of the garden are inches deep in snowdrops; so many that, following an old country-garden tradition, there are usually two dedicated Snowdrop Sundays when deliciously warming soup and snacks are served. Rivalling even the snowdrops in number, aconites add more than a touch of gold.

Tiny pink and white cyclamen, wine-dark hellebores and fragrant daphne bushes are other floral pleasures that might give these early winter-going-on-spring months the connoisseur's vote for the most delightful season of the year.

In the account of his visit, which he dictated to Samuel Pepys, King Charles II reported that, on the advice of his companion Robin Philips, he rode with him to Heale House where Mrs Hyde, whom he described as a widow gentlewoman, 'being a discreet woman, took no notice of me at the time', there being other guests present. Mrs Hyde advised the king to ride away and 'make as if I quitted the house' and return again secretly, which the king did.

Mrs Hyde, the king continued, 'told me she had a very safe place to hide me in till we knew whether our ship was ready or no… I went up into the hiding hole that was very convenient and safe, and staid there all alone… some four or five days.'

Set high on a south-facing slope at Cheddon Fitzpaine, overlooking the valley of the River Tone and with distant views of the Blackdown Hills in Somerset, are the gardens of Hestercombe House. They are one of the best surviving examples of the collaboration between Sir Edwin Lutyens and Gertrude Jekyll, built for the Honourable E W B Portman between 1903 and 1908.

The gaunt house and upper terrace were already in existence when Lutyens came to Hestercombe, and the dynamic of his design was to concentrate the garden interest to the south, fully engaging the magnificent views over the surrounding countryside. By the use of a classical open-air rotunda, he changed the direction of the 19th-century terrace to include a baroque orangery of great elegance, which he himself designed, and a Dutch garden. Lutyens used local materials, such as Morte slate from behind the house, and golden limestone from Ham Hill near Yeovil, and introduced flights of circular steps to create the feeling of spaciousness. Water, too, was used to create tranquillity, and rills run from recessed ponds – to the west through a rose garden and to the east from the rotunda pool.

From quite early in her career Miss Jekyll was extremely shortsighted, and her planting at Hestercombe and elsewhere was concerned with the texture, overall shape and perfume of plants, as well as with their colour. The Grey Walk, below the upper terrace, is planted throughout in soft colours. Greys, silver, mauve and white predominate, with lavender, rosemary and pinks interplanted with catmint.

Strongly scented choisyas are positioned at the end of the border, and yuccas and blue thistles are employed to give structure to the overall composition.

The central area has a formal layout; beds filled with pink roses contrast sharply with the strong leaves of the surrounding *Bergenia cordifolia*. Peonies, lilies and delphiniums catch the eye, and a pergola overhung with climbing roses, honeysuckle and clematis creates a fragrant as well as a colourful and shady path in summer. Characteristic of Lutyens' attention to detail are the circular windows cut in the south walls of the pergola, and the alternately square and circular pillars that support the cross-beams of the structure.

Above: The Grey Walk, planted by Gertrude Jekyll

Right: The geometric lines of the paving lead the eye to the hillside view beyond

HIDCOTE MANOR Gloucestershire GL55 6LR

4 miles (6.5km) north east of Chipping Campden | Open selected days mid-Mar to end Oct | Tel: 01386 438333 | www.nationaltrust.org.uk

Hidcote Manor Garden combines elegance with ebullience and restraint with an expression of *joie de vivre*. In keeping with the Arts and Crafts style which the garden exemplifies, there is a well-defined ground plan marked by dramatic paths, hedges in strong, straight lines and strict – though sometimes fanciful – topiary shapes. The planting is exciting and expressive, and the garden has surprises at every turn.

It was created over 100 years ago by Lawrence Johnston who, with his mother Gertrude Winthrop, bought the property in 1907 when the house was surrounded by nothing but fields and a few mature trees. Johnston read extensively, studying the work of leading garden designers, especially Gertrude Jekyll, and became a recognised horticulturist and plantsman himself. He sponsored and took part in many plant-hunting expeditions to the Alps, Kenya and South Africa and also built up a network of fellow plantsmen around the world with whom he exchanged specimen plants. As a result of these expeditions over 40 new species were cultivated in the UK, many of which bear his name, and he was awarded three Awards of Merit by the Royal Horticultural Society for his plant-hunting achievements. A yellow climbing rose he bought as an unnamed seedling from the breeder was first called 'Hidcote Yellow' but later renamed 'Lawrence Johnston'. It now garlands the north wall of the Old Garden.

Clipped hedges of holly, beech, hornbeam and yew divide the garden into separate compartments – Johnston called it a 'garden of rooms' – each with a distinctive characteristic and colour theme. The use of tapestry hedging in the Circle close to the Old Garden was innovative in garden design at the time, though mixed planting was commonplace in ancient hedgerows. Here the blend of different species such as yew, beech and holly creates an intriguingly mottled appearance which, unlike evergreen hedging, varies in colour and characteristic season by season. To further reinforce the ground plan, two axes run uncompromisingly north–south and east–west with a gazebo at their intersection.

Hedges separating the garden rooms are tall and so there is no cheating – one has to enter each room to experience the explosion of colour, the sensuous planting and the compatible marriage of formal topiary shapes and blowsy old-fashioned roses, rare shrubs and perennials.

In some cases the sense of occasion and anticipation is heightened by the style of the entrance. One of the most formal areas, the Bathing Pool garden, has a massive topiary hedge shaped in the centre to form a truly triumphal arch with a steeply pitched, overhanging roof. Its reflection in the circular pool increases the impact.

The Red Border is reached via a wide flight of stone steps flanked by a pair of tall, narrow brick pavilions with incurved roofs topped by ball-shaped finials. Pots of red geraniums and agaves on the stone walls hint at the exciting colour profusion to come.

The border is a flamboyant coming-together of red, purple, orange and bronze. The groundwork is laid with the purple-bronze foliage of *Heuchera* 'Palace Purple', which perfectly complements the 1946 blood-red floribunda *Rosa* 'Frensham', the blazing reds of *Lobelia* 'Will Scarlet' and 'Queen Victoria', *Canna indica* 'Roi Humbert' and, as always, the cherry-red verbena. A bright star in this border is the striking day lily *Hemerocallis fulva* 'Flore Pleno' with its orange-going-on-red petals the colours of leaping flames.

Inspired by designer and writer Vita Sackville-West's garden at Sissinghurst Castle in Kent, the White Garden has a billowing profusion of silver-leaved and white-flowering plants, their contrasting forms and textures linked by their uniformity of colour. The beds are bordered with low clipped hedges topped by topiary peacocks. Tall erect spires of white acanthus tower above common wormwood, *Artemisia absinthium* 'Lambrook Silver', a glorious snow-white cistus, mop-headed phlox and shrub roses. Later in the season huge clumps of white dahlias hold centre stage.

One of the glories of summer in Hidcote Manor Garden is the flourish of old roses in the Rose Walk. Johnston gradually built up a collection of 18th- and 19th-century damask, gallica and moss roses, many of which were bred in France, and planted them in two long borders. These romantic and sweetly scented roses bloom in one short-lived but exquisite midsummer burst.

'Mrs Winthrop's Garden', named after Johnston's mother, has a Mediterranean ambience and a largely blue, yellow and lime green colour theme. The edges of brick paths and a circular brick terrace are blurred by billowy hummocks of yellowy-green lady's mantle (*Alchemilla mollis*) and blue geranium. Clusters of aconitum give the scheme height and structure and terracotta pots of lemon verbena and aloe vera produce dramatic shape contrast.

Closer to the garden boundaries Johnston's planting became more cottagey, some would say jungle-like, with such delightful combinations as poppies, alliums and ferns. Azaleas and rhododendrons and rare and unusual trees are evidence of his worldwide plant quests.

Long views in the garden are scrupulously managed to enhance the wow factor of its situation in the beautiful Vale of Evesham. At the end of the Long Walk the tall iron gates are left open to frame the distant view, whilst another grass walk slopes up to the Stilt Garden, a wide avenue bordered by tall hornbeams on stilt-like trunks, surely evidence of a French influence.

In 1948 Johnston retired to Serre de la Madone, his property in the South of France, and the National Trust took over Hidcote Manor, the first gift they accepted solely because of the garden.

Fellow garden designer and passionate plantswoman Vita Sackville-West wrote of Lawrence Johnston's garden at Hidcote Manor: 'This place is a jungle of beauty. I cannot hope to describe it in words, for indeed it is an impossible thing to reproduce the shape, colour, depth and design of such a garden through the poor medium of prose.'

Left: Cosmos and dahlia flowers in September in the Old Garden with the house beyond

Below: Visitors enjoying the Red Borders in September

IFORD MANOR Wiltshire BA15 2BA

7 miles (11.25km) south east of Bath | Open selected days Apr to Oct | Tel: 01225 863146 | www.ifordmanor.co.uk

Cross the beautiful old stone bridge over the river and there is the medieval manor house with its honey-gold, 18th-century façade, nestling at the foot of the steep, wooded slopes of the Frome valley and viewed sometimes through folds of pale mauve wisteria. This initial view gives a clue to the chief elements of the garden design. Beside the house and on banks high above it are layer upon layer of trees in every shade of green, and of yellow, bronze and purple too, partially obscuring walls and subsidiary buildings.

The garden design and layout were the work of architect-turned-landscape gardener Harold Peto, who designed so many magnificent gardens in the classical manner. This, however, was his own garden, where he lived for the first three decades of the 20th century and where he created a theatrical setting for his collection of Italian Renaissance statuary and artefacts. He used the steep slope of the site to spectacular advantage, marrying structural plants and stone, and creating a series of terraces linked by flights of steps and standard Chinese wisteria shrubs (*Wisteria sinensis*). Each terrace is different from the last, each one furnished with a distinctive architectural feature – a pavilion, loggia, pool or patio – setting the stage for classical fountains, lavishly planted urns and statues.

One of these structures, on the Great Terrace, is of cathedral-like proportions and follows ecclesiastical lines. The terrace is edged with stone columns representing the nave. At the north-west end, a large semi-circular stone seat represents the apse and, continuing the ecclesiastical theme, there are two small enclosures like side chapels, one of which displays topiary emblems of the Chigi family, to whom one of the present owners, Elizabeth Cartwright-Hignett, is related.

Another architectural structure that also has its roots in ecclesiastical building design

is the Romanesque-style cloisters that Peto built in 1914 and which came to be called a 'Haunt of Ancient Peace'.

Constructed of local Westwood stone, this gloriously spiritual structure, with its arched windows and spectacular views across the valley, became a sanctuary to house many of the designer's most precious statues and other artefacts. The small inner courtyard has as the central feature an octagonal well head from a convent in the northern Italian town of Aquilegia and clematis hangs in elegant ribbons from the roof. A chapel in the cloisters was dedicated in 1916 'To the Glory of God and The Blessed Virgin Mary'.

Throughout the Grade I-listed garden, now mostly restored to Peto's design, flowers are subordinate to both architectural and clipped evergreen features. These structural plant elements are mainly designed with cypress, juniper and *Buxus sempervirens*, which grows wild in the woods above the house. There are exceptions. Banks of scented day lilies (*Hemerocallis citrina*) and naturalised martagon lilies make a glorious summer display. It is, however, the elegance of the permanent structures and the masterful use of compatible natural materials that make this garden seem aloof from the changing seasons. The garden he created for his own home at Iford Manor is considered one of Peto's finest Italianate gardens.

A son of Sir Samuel Morton Peto, who built the Houses of Parliament and Nelson's Column in London, Harold Ainsworth Peto (1854–1933) became a partner in an architectural practice in London in 1876, where for one year in 1880 Edwin Lutyens was a pupil. Peto, by then a collector and connoisseur of Italian landscape and art and an exact contemporary of Gertrude Jekyll, the eminent garden designer, left the partnership in the 1890s and became one of the foremost landscape gardeners of his time.

Left: The Peto garden, with elegant urns and classical statuary

Above: Harold Peto used the steep slope of the site to spectacular advantage

The roof space at Iford Mill Barn has the distinction of becoming the summer breeding roost for a colony of greater horseshoe bats, one of the few known roosts for this species to survive in England. With over 250 individual greater horseshoe bats recorded in the barn each summer, the buildings and a small area of land surrounding them were designated, in 1996, Sites of Special Scientific Interest (SSSIs).

Spring comes early and winter is soon forgotten in the West Country where the castle stands on the Ince peninsula, a promontory jutting out into the tidal St Germans River. The gardens herald this seasonal advance with waves of hellebores, primroses and spring bulbs – purple, mauve and blue, pink, yellow and white – covering glades and woodlands and lining paths and driveways. And then in summer there is a seasonal drift too, when borders are a luxuriant tapestry of mixed colours, and wild flower meadows lead the eye to the inlet where sailing boats bob on the water.

Left: A delightful little drummer boy garlanded in ivy

Above: A stone sphinx gazes out to sea from a tulip-filled flower meadow

When Lord and Lady Boyd – Simon Boyd is the second Viscount – moved into the property in 1994, Alice Boyd 'inherited' a garden laid out and tended for over three decades by her mother-in-law. The protecting belt of trees, a necessary precaution on this wind- and salt-lashed site, was already in place, some probably dating back to the early 19th century. Many of the outer rims consisting mainly of leylandii have recently been removed as other species have developed enough to take over the protection role. A recent addition, two rows of evergreen oaks, will eventually form a tunnel beside the summer garden.

The shortness and relative warmth of the Cornish winters mean that this is not ideal territory for herbaceous plants; they do not have a long enough period of dormancy. For this reason Alice Boyd plants borders with

a dense foundation of evergreen shrubs and then adds annuals, half-hardy annuals, bulbs and some perennials. The effect is of profusion, luxuriance and a gloriously harmonious colour mix in the English country garden tradition.

Borders throughout the garden are at their peak from July until October and now, because of Alice Boyd's plant selection, usually until well into November. In one border there are recurring clusters of foliage plants such as the variegated *Salvia officinalis* 'Icterina', its pale green-and-yellow leaves providing a light background for more showy salvias including the bright blue *Salvia patens* and the gloriously rich and fragrant chocolate cosmos, *Cosmos atrosanguineus,* which flowers late into the autumn.

The deep red and russet tones of autumn foliage are a recurring theme in the late-

flowering borders. The arching stems of dark orange crocosmia, scarlet and ruby red dahlias and yellow and orange kniphofia mingle with annual sunflowers in colours from deep rust to bright gold. Punctuating this abundance of flower colour there are clumps of the castor oil plant, *Ricinus communis,* whose large glossy leaves give solidity and structure to the planting.

The walled garden which is still part kitchen garden, part orchard has more borders, particularly resplendent in summer when a purple, magenta and lime green colour scheme is effected with deep mauve buddleia, catmint *Nepeta x faassenii*, the dark-flowered *Geranium psilostemon* and the refreshingly yellowy-green *Euphorbia schillingii* and lady's mantle, *Alchemilla mollis*

A terrace around the house is gradually becoming less well defined as self-seeding plants are welcome to stay. These include fat, round hummocks of the white, pink and purple daisy-like flowers of *Erigeron karvinskianus* and the tall, swaying stems of purple-violet *Verbena bonariensis*. A once-straight inlaid pebble path leading past a sundial is similarly invaded, now encroached on both sides by dense planting of shrub roses, cistus, nicotiana and geraniums. The focal point of the terrace is an 18th-century fountain and, to one side of it, a magnificent Australian leptospermum tree covered in early summer with flowers the colour of ripe watermelon.

Throughout the garden there are elegant and intriguing surprises. A beautiful stone seat nestles in a border beside a wide grass path, and an old stone wall running parallel with the river would not look out of place in a cottage garden, as orange eschscholzia, pink hedera and lilac mallow form clumps over and around it. In the midst of a grass and wild flower meadow, where the garden appears to merge into the shoreline, the bust

Above: Practical recycling: rustic seating in the orchard

Top right: A corbelled arch framing a glorious golden tree

Right: The folly, whose interior walls are covered with intricate panels and mosaics

of a stone angel rises gracefully from a sea of ox-eye daisies, knapweed and bird's foot trefoil.

Most intriguing of all is the small tower-like folly which stands at one end of a narrow rectangular pool. The interior walls are completely covered with intricate panels of shells, stones, cross-sections of minerals and other *objets trouvés*, a glowing, iridescent mural of items collected by Simon Boyd's father, Alan Lennox-Boyd, who was Secretary of State for the Colonies in the 1950s and who became the first Viscount Boyd.

He and his wife Lady Patricia Boyd bought Ince Castle in 1960 but it was not until 1995 when Simon and Alice Boyd lowered the ground to the east of the property that the spectacular shoreline could be seen from the house. Now, on the horizon in one direction it is possible to see Plymouth and in the other direction, over the water, there is a pastoral scene of patchwork fields, pinewoods and cottages watched over by two sphinxes.

The glorious red-flowering tree close to the terrace at Ince Castle is one of a genus native to south-east Australia and New Zealand, where it is known as the tea tree. It is said that Captain Cook infused the leaves to make a tea-like drink. The tree, which has small, evergreen leaves, can grow to a height of 50 feet (15 metres). It can withstand strong winds but needs the protection of other trees from maritime exposure.

A castellated manor house rather than a true castle, Ince Castle has four three-storey towers, battlements, and walls 4 feet (1.2 metres) thick. It was built at the beginning of the Civil War in 1642 for Henry Killigrew, the Royalist Member of Parliament for Looe in Cornwall. The property was later run as a farm and by the late 19th century had fallen into disrepair. Severe fire damage in 1988 necessitated the rebuilding of the roof.

KIFTSGATE COURT
Gloucestershire GL55 6LN

3 miles (5km) north east of Chipping Campden | **Open selected afternoons Apr to Sep** | **Tel: 01386 438777** | **www.kiftsgate.co.uk**

Situated high up in the Cotswold Hills above the Vale of Evesham, Kiftsgate has natural advantages of topography which, in the past, have been enhanced by its proximity to the great garden of Hidcote. It is, perhaps, rare to find two such fine gardens so close together, but Heather Muir, who built the Kiftsgate gardens from 1920, was a close friend of Lawrence Johnston, the creator of Hidcote, and Kiftsgate undoubtedly benefited from Major Johnston's plant-hunting expeditions to Japan and China. Today, the gardens are beautifully maintained by Heather Muir's grand-daughter, Mrs A H Chambers, and her husband, and some of

the unusual plants to be seen in the gardens are available in the plant sales area.

From the terrace there are spectacular views over the countryside to the Malvern Hills, and the edge is guarded by a splendid rose, 'Frühlingsgold', which has abundant blooms in June. In spring the White Sunk Garden is a mass of flowering bulbs, and its wide beds are full of shrubs intended to provide a year-round display of colour. Among the white roses is *Rosa sericea* 'Heather Muir', a single, early-flowering shrub which grows up to 12 feet (3.5 metres) in height, but the glory of the rose border is *R. filipes* 'Kiftsgate', a white rose which,

when last measured, was 80 feet (24 metres) by 90 feet (27 metres) with a height of 50 feet (15 metres).

Among other notable features of Kiftsgate are the perennial geraniums, a large wisteria and some large species of hydrangea. Equally attractive is a small enclosure, approached beneath a whitebeam archway, which is devoted to ferns and ornamental grasses. The most recent addition to the garden is a minimalist Water Garden whose simplicity and calm contrast with the abundance of the main garden.

As you descend the hill to the Lower Garden, down a steep path, there are tall Monterey pines which provide shelter for the tender shrubs that thrive in these protected conditions.

Left: The White Sunk Garden

Right: Temple and pool in the Lower Garden

Below: Minimalist sculpture in the Water Garden

KNIGHTSHAYES COURT Devon EX16 7RQ

2 miles (3km) north of Tiverton | Usually open daily mid-Mar to end Oct | Tel: 01884 254665 | **www.nationaltrust.org.uk**

Deep in the luxuriant Devon countryside north of Tiverton is one of last century's great gardens. The house at Knightshayes was designed in typically eccentric style by William Burges in 1869 and the framework of the garden established at that time by Edward Kemp, but it was Sir John and Lady Heathcoat Amory who undertook the planning and planting from 1945. Now owned by the National Trust, the 50-acre (20ha) garden is, perhaps, most famous for the Paved and Pool Gardens and for the beautiful Garden in a Wood, created by Sir Eric Savill and Norman Hadden and regarded by many as their masterpiece.

The garden at Knightshayes is approached through the former stable block, which today serves as the Trust's shop, restaurant and plant nursery, and then via the north-western corner of the house towards the conservatory. Against the house is a magnificent *Magnolia grandiflora* 'Exmouth', and a quince which produces large red flowers during the spring and spherical yellow fruits. From this top terrace you can appreciate the way in which the garden relates directly to the countryside to the south; at the end of the terrace a border includes dianthus, artemisias and veronicas, as well as an attractive mauve sage.

Beyond a short flight of steps there is a yew hedge sculpted by Sir Ian Heathcoat Amory to form a hunting scene in topiary, and raised beds of alpines lead into the Paved Garden. The theme of this striking 'garden room' is silver, with dwarf geraniums breaking up the harsh pattern of the paving. There is also a fine lead cistern filled with plants. Assisted by the late Lanning Roper, Sir John and Lady Heathcoat Amory have transformed a bowling green into a serene water garden featuring a circular waterlily pool. It is surrounded by battlemented yew hedges and a single weeping pear which

contrasts with the late summer leaves of an *Acer pseudoplatanus* 'Brilliantissimum' peering over the hedge.

The Garden in a Wood is a triumph of balance. The beeches, oaks and larches have been carefully thinned to let in sufficient light to enable bold-coloured and delicately shaded rhododendrons and azaleas to flower; the effect is enhanced by the brilliant underplanting of crocus, narcissus, cyclamen and trilliums. Hostas, irises and euphorbias also flourish, and there are sun-lovers, such as astelias from New Zealand, as well as climbing roses, honeysuckle and clematis.

Beyond the wood is an open lawn planted with birch, a glade, and a lower border holding sages, hostas and meconopsis. Sir John's Wood has many larches and evergreens, while the extension to the South Garden includes a number of striking dogwoods, as well as Japanese cherries which give dramatic colour in spring.

Another gem within the property is the stunning ornamental Victorian Walled Kitchen Garden. Fully restored in 2003, this south-easterly sloping site is divided into eight beds, four of which are used for growing a rotation of annual vegetable crops, whilst the other four are planted with more permanent crops including vines, asparagus, artichokes and fruit. The whole garden is managed on organic principles and the produce is used in the Knightshayes restaurant as well as being sold to visitors from one of the garden's turrets and also in a local market.

LOST GARDENS OF HELIGAN Cornwall PL26 6EN

4 miles (6.5km) south of St Austell | Open daily except 24-25 Dec | Tel: 01726 845100 | www.heligan.com

Heligan, seat of the Tremayne family for more than 400 years, is one of the most mysterious estates in England. At the end of the 19th century its 1,000 acres (405ha) were at their zenith, but only a few years after the Great War of 1914–18 bramble and ivy were already drawing a green veil over this 'Sleeping Beauty'. After decades of neglect its restoration was commenced by a small band of enthusiasts, so successfully that Heligan was voted the Nation's Favourite Garden by BBC *Gardeners' World* and now offers 200 acres (81ha) open for the public to explore.

Heligan's Victorian Productive Gardens are once again intensively cultivated throughout the year, growing over 200 varieties of heritage fruit and vegetables. Thanks to the crop introductions of the plant hunters and the Victorian revolution in garden technology, pineapples, citrus, melons and peaches were home-grown for luxury consumption. Today, the Paxton glasshouses, cold frames and manure-heated pineapple pit produce a similar cornucopia of crops.

First laid out over two centuries ago, the Pleasure Grounds conceal an unusual series of romantic structures and unexpected features, including restored New Zealand and Italian gardens; summerhouses and pools; a superb pre-Jekyll herbaceous border; a rocky ravine; and a crystal grotto and wishing well. A network of walks, lined by magnificent historic flowering shrubs, links these special places. Heligan's ancient rhododendron and camellia collections will not survive for much longer, but as over-mature specimens they hold an awesome and captivating grace.

The exuberant 'Jungle' garden hosts a riot of luxuriant foliage, sub-tropical plantings and specimen trees. Set in the micro-climate of a steep-sided valley, the boardwalk snakes down through bamboo tunnels, palm-lined avenues, around four ponds and a cascading stream, enticing the visitor on a journey that seems far from our temperate shores; one loses oneself amid almost prehistoric tree ferns, giant rhubarb, succulents and banana palms.

Visitors are invited to wander through woodland and take farm walks across the beautiful Cornish countryside, where sustainable management practices promote habitat conservation and a pioneering wildlife project offers an unforgettable close-up view of native wildlife.

The variety of habitats throughout the gardens and estate provides a breadth of seasonal interest, including spring flowers, mosses and lichens, ferns and autumn fungi, as well as a considerable range of resident and visiting birds, owls, bats, butterflies and moths, insects, reptiles and small mammals.

Left: The moss-covered sleeping Mud Maid was created by local artists Sue Hill and her brother Pete

Below: The boardwalk leads visitors through areas of luxuriant sub-tropical plantings with the ambience of faraway places

SNOWSHILL MANOR Glos WR12 7JU

3 miles (5km) south of Broadway | Open selected days Apr to early Dec | Tel: 01386 852410 | www.nationaltrust.org.uk

Situated on a Cotswold hillside with spectacular views over some of the most beautiful countryside in Gloucestershire, Snowshill Manor gardens were built as a series of interconnecting 'rooms', in the same way as Hidcote Manor gardens (see page 32). The then owner, Charles Wade, was himself an architect and a devotee of the Arts and Crafts ideals popularised by William Morris, and in 1919 he commissioned another architect of like mind, M H Baillie Scott, to transform what he called 'a wilderness of chaos' into the series of terraces, the Armillary Court, the shrubbery and the Well Garden, as well as the kitchen gardens we see now.

Wade was an obsessive collector of items of craftsmanship – bicycles, musical instruments, clocks, Chinese lacquer cabinets, and many other works of art, which he placed in the manor house, although he himself actually lived in a small cottage called The Priest's House until his death in 1956. Today, Snowshill is owned by the National Trust, which displays Wade's eccentric collections and maintains the charming country garden to its usual high standard.

To the left of the terrace garden there is a beautiful double border, one side of which is bright with red Oriental and yellow Welsh poppies. On the other wall climbers are artfully trained, while the bold lines of espaliered figs stand out in tempting fashion.

Charles Wade had a special love of the colour blue, and seats and woodwork throughout the gardens at Snowshill are painted with a particular shade now known as 'Wade' blue – a powdery dark blue with a touch of turquoise. There can be no doubt that this blue harmonises well with the Cotswold stone walls, and is a particularly attractive colour in a landscape setting. It also provides a sympathetic foil for the mauves and purples which are used to such good effect. In adopting this as his 'signature' colour for the garden furniture, Wade asserted that there was no shade of green paint that could possibly match the magnificent hues of nature.

A spring rising under the manor house feeds several small basins, a fountain and pools. Behind one of the former cow byres is a tall, white guelder rose, *Vibernum opulus*, underplanted with ferns. As you climb

the steps near the shrubbery the path is overhung with weeping white mulberries, and there is a strong atmosphere here of the Victorian romantic garden.

For almost two decades the garden at Snowshill has been managed without the use of any chemicals, relying on wildlife to maintain a perfect natural balance.

Natural feeds are used, composed of seaweed extract, blood, fish and bone, and Snowshill's home-grown compost has an added special ingredient: dove excrement from the dovecote. Bees and other beneficial insects are attracted into the garden by the

Far left: Blue paintwork brightens the Well Court with its sunken pond and Mr Wade's cottage

Left: Bright pink phlox provides colour at the arched gateway between the Long Border and the Armillary Court

Above: The garden in July

judicious planting of nectar-rich species including alliums, asters, echium, marigolds, mignonette and sedums. In turn, they earn their keep by feeding on the aphids and other pests.

Areas along the visitor route to the manor are planted with British natural shrubs that produce early blossom, nuts or fruits or provide habitat for birds and small mammals.

These include sloe, hawthorn, elderberry and spindleberry, guelder rose, wild roses, dogwood and field maple.

Visitors to the garden, who might previously have been unaware of these specific planting plans, are almost certain to notice the joyous variety of the bird song and the friendly hum of the bees as they wander through the grounds.

t says much for the charm and beauty of Stourton House Flower Gardens that they stand comparison with the magnificent landscaped grounds of Stourhead situated only a matter of 300 yards (274 metres) away. In 4½ acres (2ha) there are countless plant treasures accommodated in a series of small,

Stourton is also a garden with a purpose: it produces flowers and foliage for drying, with up to 70 per cent of the perennial plants being used for drying and composing into beautiful, lasting bouquets.

There is an interesting historical connection between the two gardens. In late

one of the daughters of the Hoare family at Stourhead. Money from the wealthy banking family went into the construction of Stourton House, laying out a garden and planting a run of what are now magnificent trees. However, it was not until the late Colonel and Mrs Elizabeth Bullivant came to live here in 1957

Left: Hosta in full flower near beautiful blue hydrangea 'Vicomtesse de Vibraye'

Right: Many of the 270 varieties of hydrangea displayed around the garden are bred there

the house that the garden began to take on its present character.

Now the main gardens lie to the east of the house and visitors are recommended to start their tour in the Kitchen Garden where the beds contain not only vegetables but also a range of flowers suitable for drying, including annual poppies, lady's mantle (*Alchemilla mollis*), teasels and other wild flowers. Here you will also see some of the 270 varieties of hydrangea, blues and whites, creams and pinks, many of them extremely rare, for which Stourton House is famous.

On either side of the path leading down to the beautifully sculpted Hedged Garden is an avenue of cypresses (*Leylandii* 'Herculaneum') known as the Twelve Apostles. The central pool is surrounded by beds of shrubs and herbaceous plants while the stone flower fountain in the centre is filled with seasonal-flowering plants. The water-loving plants around the pool include the carnivorous pitcher plants, flowering rushes and groups of water iris, both yellow and purple. Around the margins are rock roses, alchemillas and geraniums whilst the surrounding beds are overflowing with tree peonies, hydrangeas, roses, honesty, meadowfoam and wild flowers that offer colour and food for butterflies, bees and birds throughout the season.

To the south of the Hedged Garden is the Lower Pond Garden. In spring unique daffodils and narcissus surround the home-bred Award of Merit *Viburnum plicatum*

f. 'Elizabeth Bullivant' which has lacy white flowers in May. This beautiful shrub flowers for a second time in September when, spectacularly, it is also covered in scarlet berries. Nearby there is a pocket handkerchief tree, *Davidia involucrata*, a splendid *Magnolia liliiflora* 'Nigra', which boasts purple flowers, and an enormous eucalyptus tree.

Beyond the south lawn and the 19th-century greenhouse, perhaps a relic of the link with the Hoare family, is a massive red rhododendron sheltering erythroniums and fritillary and in the Secret Garden there are many May-flowering rhododendrons and scented azaleas. On the west side of the garden, part of the paddock was turned into additional shrubbery under the beautiful copper beech trees. It has been planted with a tulip tree, many varieties of rhododendron, azalea, camellia, pieris and, for late-summer flowering, wonderful, graceful hydrangeas in many colours.

This is a fascinating, romantic, natural garden with meandering paths beneath wisteria, honeysuckle and roses. The different 'rooms' give constant surprise and interest. Many plants, like the brightly coloured wild flowers, have self-seeded to give Stourton House garden a combination that is a challenge to achieve: that of a true cottage garden together with a feeling of structure and formality.

Cream teas with a difference are a speciality of the house. On a July afternoon you might be lucky enough to be served light-as-air scones with home-made rose petal jam and a scattering of rose petals.

Top left: Red lacecap 'Geoffrey Chadbund'

Left: Shapes and textures create maximum effect

Right: This quintessentially English country garden has colour, fragrance and tranquillity

TINTINHULL HOUSE Somerset BA22 8PZ

4 miles (6.5km) north west of Yeovil | Open selected days mid-Mar to end Oct | Tel: 01935 823289 | www.nationaltrust.org.uk

The layout at Tintinhull House is aesthetically pleasing. The garden here so perfectly complements the 1630 house that one feels that the design must be contemporary, and yet it was created during the last century, largely by Mrs Phyllis Reiss who lived here for 28 years. Then again, so skilful is the arrangement of walled and hedged enclosures, the placing of important trees, and the vistas that the garden seems much larger than its 2 acres (1ha). Add to these

remarkable qualities borders planted for all-year-round interest and designed with the texture and shape of plants in mind and it is clear that, perhaps due in no small way to the acclaimed garden writer Penelope Hobhouse, who lived here until 1993, Tintinhull is one of the most interesting gardens to be found in the south of England.

The main axis of the garden runs from the five-bayed west front of the house through three compartments to the western

boundary, while a path crosses this line at the fountain and passes through the Kitchen Garden to the orchard. Further strong design elements are provided by the great Cedar of Lebanon in Cedar Court, which is a broad, asymmetrical shape, and the two mighty holm oaks that interrupt the view to the south west and create the backdrop to the Pool Garden.

The garden can be approached either from the house or by way of the north front

above Cedar Court, through an arch. The four plots are planted with regal lilies that flower in early summer and with box domes which have been in their present positions since the 1930s. On the north side are choisyas, honeysuckles, roses, agapanthus and rosemary, while on the west there are several varieties of clematis and tree peonies. To the south, begonias and a perennial honesty predominate, and on the east side are lovely groups of lavender, including 'Hidcote', a variety named after the garden that has provided so much of the inspiration for Tintinhull.

The central garden has a further series of box domes, but here hydrangeas and roses are the main features. Azaleas are planted in beds on either side of the central path in the next enclosure, which in spring and early summer is alive with colourful bulbs, including *Anemone apennina*.

The Pool Garden and its pavilion were constructed by Mrs Reiss in 1947 to commemorate her nephew, a fighter pilot who was killed in action over Malta during World War II.

The west border is a riot of hot colours that contrast strikingly with the border on the other side of the canal, where soft pale greys and silver foliage predominate.

Young visitors, especially, delight in the bird-feeding area, and even the car park has its attractions. It is set among picturesque orchards and, beyond, there are farm animals grazing in the paddock.

Left: The Kitchen Garden is planted with fragrant catmint and honeysuckle

Above: The Pool Garden is enlivened by pink, crimson and yellow waterlilies, and by yellow iris reflected at the corners

TREBAH GARDEN Cornwall TR11 5JZ

3 miles (5km) south of Falmouth | Usually open daily all year | Tel: 01326 252200 | www.trebahgarden.co.uk

Even by Cornish standards, the gardens of Trebah are quite remarkable. Covering 25 acres (10ha), they occupy a ravine running from a fine 18th-century house at its head down to a private beach on the Helford River, dropping more than 200 feet (61 metres) in the process.

Its original creator, Charles Fox, came to Trebah in 1826, and to shelter the ravine from the fierce coastal winds he planted a great screen of maritime pines, *Pinus pinaster*, behind which seeds and plants collected from all over the world could flourish.

A stream runs through a water garden in the upper part of Trebah, created since 1981 by the present owners, Major and Mrs Hibbert. Small pools edged with primulas and water irises, astilbes and ligularias, bamboo and ferns give colour and form to the scene, while the lower part of the ravine supports the largest *Gunnera manicata* (Brazilian rhubarb) that most people are likely to see.

A dense network of paths leads either down into the valley, just a short way down to the Koi Pool and waterfall, or along the Camellia Walk to a viewpoint overlooking the beach. Below, there are many spring- and early summer-flowering species of rhododendron. Some, including 'Trebah Gem', which was planted in 1900, have now reached 45 feet (13 metres) in height, while two 'Loderi King George' have delicate pink buds which open in May as large white, fragrant blooms.

Trebah is famous for its tender trees and shrubs. A large Chilean laurel with bright green, aromatic leaves can be seen in the Chilean Combe, and the dogwood, 'Bentham's Cornel', with its yellow bracts, does well. Magnolias, including *Magnolia x soulangiana*, and the pink tulip tree are also well represented, as are many varieties of eucalyptus, pieris and tree fern. Two extremely tall Chusan palm trees dominate the view down the ravine, and you can also see a pocket handkerchief tree and an exotic though actually quite hardy Chinese fir. Alas, when temperatures fell to −15°C (5°F) in January 1987, Trebah lost many beautiful trees, including the largest *Eucalyptus ovata* in England and a *Rhododendron sinogrande*, thought to be more than 100 years old.

Care has been taken to extend the flowering season through to Christmas; a bonus for the visitor that has been achieved with acres of blue and white hydrangeas.

Below: An impressive panoramic view of *Gunnera manicata* in the valley

Right: The Koi Pool and waterfall, lively with fish

TRESCO ABBEY
Tresco, Isles of Scilly TR24 0QQ

Usually open daily | Tel: 01720 424108 | www.tresco.co.uk

Few gardens are reached by a more exciting journey than the Abbey Gardens on Tresco, one of the Isles of Scilly. There is a choice of either taking the *Scillonian* ferry from Penzance, and then a launch from St Mary's, or a helicopter – also from Penzance – that goes direct to the garden gates. The gardens are a remarkable work of construction by their founder, Augustus Smith, in 1834, and they are maintained today by his descendant, the present owner, R A Dorrien Smith.

Tresco lies in the Atlantic 30 miles (48km) off the coast of Cornwall and is warmed by the Gulf Stream. Although the temperatures in winter rarely fall below 10°C (50°F), exceptional sub-zero temperatures in January 1987 caused terrible damage to some of the sub-tropical plants. Of course, the wind is an ever-present enemy, and with great forethought, Augustus Smith gave his three great terraces, the Long Walk and the Middle and Top Terraces, shelter-belts of Monterey cypress, tall hedges of holm oak and high retaining walls. These also provide an effective setting for the granite house that he built near the ruins of a Benedictine priory.

The 14-acre (5.5ha) gardens are home to many exotic plants, including the South African proteus, the tender geranium from Madeira, *G. maderense*, tall date palms from the Canary Islands and the striking Chilean *Myrtus luma* which has orange-coloured bark. There are also acacias, eucalyptus and the New Zealand *Metrosideros tomentosa*, which is 80 feet (24 metres) tall, has a great number of aerial roots and produces crimson flowers in summer.

Around St Nicholas's Priory, honeysuckles, the blue-flowering *Convolvulus mauritanicus* and the pretty Mexican daisy spill out of cracks in the ancient walls and arches, and there is a magnificent rock garden excavated

Left: Plants grow out of every nook and cranny of the priory's ancient archways

Above: Shell mosaic on a floral theme

Right: The magnificent date palms in the Abbey gardens, seen at their best against a brilliant blue sky

into a 40-foot (12-metre) cliff below. The Middle Terrace has an area known as Mexico, and is covered with the turquoise flowers of *Puya alpestris* from Chile. Further along, a stone summerhouse is overgrown with Burmese honeysuckle.

Tresco Abbey gardens offer many unusual delights, but no visitor should miss the so-called Valhalla. Open on one side, this fascinating building houses some of the figureheads of ships that have tragically foundered on the treacherous rocks around the Isles of Scilly in the course of the last three centuries.

TREWITHEN GARDENS Cornwall TR2 4DD

The word 'Trewithen' is Cornish for 'House in the Spinney', and the mature trees of the 18th-century park have undoubtedly offered protection from the coastal winds, enabling many tender plants to flourish here.

George Johnstone inherited the property in 1904 and devoted the rest of his life to creating and maintaining the 28-acre (11ha) garden, which occupies a level site 250 feet (76 metres) above sea level. A great hybridist, he played an important part in the development of the popular *Camellia x williamsii* 'Donation', but his first love was magnolias, and the Royal Horticultural Society published his magisterial work, *Asiatic Magnolias in Cultivation*, in 1955. Many of Johnstone's plants are still to be seen today at Trewithen, and this wonderful garden is now owned by his grandson, Michael Galsworthy.

It is ironic that The Glade, perhaps the most admired part of Trewithen, came about as a result of a government order during World War I to fell 300 trees.

The lawn stretches for over 200 yards (183 metres) to the south of the house, but the first part of this magnificent amphitheatre is dominated by one of the garden's great trees, *Magnolia campbellii mollicomata*, more than 55 feet (17 metres) high and covered with large pink blooms in early March. Close to it is the tulip tree, whose blooms are a slightly deeper shade of pink, while other favourites to be admired include *M. liliiflora*, with purplish pink flowers, and *M. x soulangiana*.

Further south is a group of hybrid rhododendrons, including 'Alison Johnstone' (named after George Johnstone's wife); the Chilean fire bush, which turns completely scarlet in May; a coral-bark maple; and a fine southern beech – a conical tree whose leaves change to orange and red in autumn. Camellias play an important part in the

Woodland Garden to the west of The Glade lawn. 'Trewithen Pink' can be seen, as can 'Elizabeth Johnstone', named after the Johnstones' daughter, and a camellia with a single pink bloom named after the present owner's late wife, 'Charlotte Galsworthy'. Shrubs, including viburnums, azaleas, potentillas, euonymus and berberis, edge the lawn in front of the house.

The Walled Garden, which is covered with tender plants, surrounds a pool, while a wisteria-draped pergola adds colour to this formal area. Recently planted beds of birch and sorbus, mahonia, dogwoods and roses, heathers and conifers help to make Trewithen a garden not only with an outstanding plant collection, but a place of ever-changing variety and colour.

Left: Candle primulas planted to magnificent effect

Above: Foliage and flowers in inspirational borders

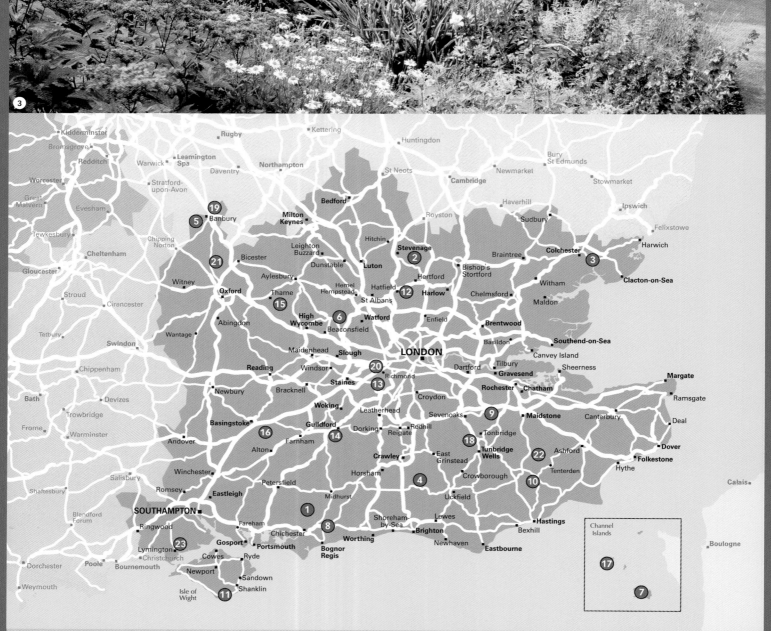

SOUTH & SOUTH EAST ENGLAND | 2

The South and South East of the country is a pleasing mixture of diverse landscapes. The gardens in this region range from welcome oases on the urban fringes of London and the home counties to those tucked away in the rural heart of Hampshire. The chapter opens with a reconstructed medieval cottage garden displaying the practical and pretty planting plan that endures in many of Britain's country gardens to this day. This chapter also includes country gardens with a slightly more exotic flavour; perhaps because of their location in the Channel Islands and the Isle of Wight. Gardens created by some of the most influential designers of recent times – the faithful restoration of a Gertrude Jekyll creation, Christopher Lloyd's iconic and innovative Sussex garden at Great Dixter and Vita Sackville-West's world-renowned Kentish masterpiece – feature alongside others also created with expertise and individuality.

18

10

BAYLEAF FARMSTEAD

West Sussex PO18 0EU

7 miles (11.25km) north of Chichester | Usually open daily | Tel: 01243 811348 | www.wealddown.co.uk

Peas and beans, pot marigolds and poppies, winter savory and thyme, woven wattle fences and a well for water – the garden around the Bayleaf Farmstead is a nostalgic and authentic look back in time to cottage gardens over four centuries ago, when vegetables, edible flowers and weeds grew higgledy-piggledy together creating unintentional drifts of colour.

The 15th-century Kentish house, rescued from the site of a new reservoir, has been re-erected as part of the Weald and Downland Open Air Museum, where events held throughout the year give a further insight into the daily lives of our ancestors.

Cottage gardens at the time were devoted to the intensive cultivation of fruit and vegetables, herbs and some flowers, both for the household kitchen and medicinal use. Space was not spared for decorative pathways and terraces; structural features such as fences, shelters and plant supports were made from wood cut from copses and hedgerows.

This is how the Bayleaf garden has been planned. Fences and low edging panels have been woven from wattle. Slender branches are tied together as plant supports for peas and beans and an open shelter storing tools, implements and beehives is reinforced with

thin branches. Hedgerow roses clambering over the front are merely decorative. Beside the shelter and a short distance from the house there is a brick well of the kind that would have been used to draw water for the house and garden.

The main vegetables grown in cottage gardens in medieval times were brassicas such as borecole and coleworts (types of loose-leaf kale) and roots including turnips and skirrets, which tasted like watery parsnips, together with leeks, onions, spinach beet, peas, beans, Alexanders ('poor man's celery') and lettuce. Many of the greens would have been used to make a boiled pottage or soup. Herbs such as parsley and sage and flowers including pot marigolds and feverfew were used for flavouring and for tisanes (teas) and ointments. Tansy and wormwood were grown as strewing herbs for the house, to help deter insects.

From time to time there are cookery demonstrations at the museum showing how the garden produce would have been cooked, and occasional 'herb days' showing, for example, how to make calendula ointment from marigolds.

In the height of summer the Bayleaf garden seems to invite the medieval housewife to wander out of doors with her flat basket to pick the peas growing amongst the flowers and edible weeds, or to gather

handfuls of fresh herbs to add flavour and variety to the kitchen pot.

Other herbs and flowers, including rosemary, sage, thyme and marigolds, would be picked and used to make decorative and fragrant tussie-mussies – small, loosely tied posies – to scent and freshen the rooms in the homestead.

As the summer wore on, she would supplement gooseberries, raspberries and wild strawberries from the garden with blackberries and bullace (wild plums) from the hedgerows and, later, in the autumn months, gather apples and pears from the orchard to store away for the coming winter.

There were once many shaws – small woodlands – growing around Bayleaf

Farmstead in its original Weald of Kent location, and three have now been planted at the museum with similar trees and shrubs. Oak and ash are the main timber trees planted, with other species including hazel, hawthorn and field maple.

As these shaws grow and develop they will not only create an authentic landscape but – notionally at least – be able to provide timber and saplings for structural work around the farmstead.

Left: A profusion of poppies growing in front of the reconstructed 15th-century Kentish house

Below: Feverfew marigolds add splashes of colour between the large colewort leaves

BENINGTON LORDSHIP Hertfordshire SG2 7BS

4 miles (6.5km) east of Stevenage | **Open some days in Feb for snowdrops and selected days** | **Tel: 08701 261709** | **www.beningtonlordship.co.uk**

Situated near Stevenage, Benington Lordship occupies a site that has been inhabited since the time of the Norman Conquest, and can boast a keep which dates from the 11th century, a moat which is covered with snowdrops in early spring, fine views over the surrounding countryside and glorious herbaceous borders.

In 1905, when the present owner's great-grandfather, Arthur Bott, bought the property, there was no garden, and the area now occupied by the park and garden was a nine-hole golf course. As well as enlarging the house, Arthur Bott created a garden with a characteristic Edwardian flavour which is still maintained by Mr and Mrs R R A Bott and their gardener, Richard Webb.

Benington Lordship stands on heavy clay 400 feet (122 metres) above sea level, so that the beds have to be heavily mulched with compost and manure. Much of the grass is not cut until the full summer when the leaves have died, and in consequence the gardens are famous for their spring colour, with drifts of snowdrops, scillas, cowslips and garlic. Further winter interest is currently being added with the planting of cornus and hellebores.

It is the profusion of naturalised snowdrops that puts the Benington Lordship garden on the 'must see' list for visitors as spring approaches. One can wander past the carpets of snowflake-white flowers

that cover the moat and surround the Norman castle and the house and perceive them as, well, just a brilliant floriferous carpet. Prolific in these areas are the single *Galanthus nivalis* and the double *G. nivalis* 'Flore Pleno', but it is in the mature shrub borders of the Walled Garden – where new borders are constantly being added – that one can appreciate collections of hundreds of named and labelled varieties; compare, perhaps, those with intriguing names such as 'Grumpy', 'Blewbury Tart', 'Carpentry Shop', 'Daphne's Scissors' and many more. Recently an unusual yellow form of *G. nivalis* was found growing near the ruin, and around the fruit trees in the pool area there is *G.* 'Mighty Atom', notable for flowers up to 2 inches

(5cm) across and, by contrast, the dainty *G. gracilis* 'Highdown' which has twisted blue leaves and finely marked flowers.

In front of the house, the Rose Garden has been replanted with, among others, the fragrant, bluish-white rose 'Margaret Merril' and with 'Radox Bouquet'. Along the verandah, which recalls Arthur Bott's time in India, is a collection of roses. From the west end of the house there are splendid views over the old entrance drive, and a large urn, found in the moat, has been surrounded by a camomile lawn. Beyond the urn, past a number of crab apple trees and cowslip banks, a path leads to the moat.

Set surprisingly far away from the house, two wonderfully deep borders run east to

west below the Kitchen Garden, which still grows a wide variety of vegetables and herbs. Interrupted by fine, brick gate piers, the borders are bright in summer with rock roses, sedums, salvias and potentillas. They are backed by further beds full of wonderful autumn colour, one overflowing with Michaelmas daisies, a plant popular in Edwardian times when this beautiful garden was created.

Left: A view across the moat to the early 18th-century house at Benington Lordship, which is renowned for its display of many varieties of snowdrop in February and early March

Above: Almost up to their necks in snow!

BETH CHATTO GARDENS

No one who has seen Beth Chatto's display gardens at the Chelsea Flower Show can doubt that she is one of the most influential gardeners of our time, and a visit to her own gardens at Elmstead Market more than confirms this view. In her book *The Dry Garden*, Beth Chatto emphasises that she selects each plant or tree 'for its shape and character, not for the colour of its flowers', and this respect for the habit of plants is the dominant impression you gain on entering the gardens.

Before 1960 there was neither house nor garden on the site, and with just a few trees in place, Beth Chatto gradually converted the problem areas into gardens of different characters: the dry gravel parts are filled with drought-resistant plants bright with warm colours; a woodland garden lies in the shade of tall trees; and water gardens have been made where it was boggy before. These distinct types of garden now show an astonishing range of plants.

Initially, Mr and Mrs Chatto tackled the gravel areas which surround the house, and constructed the Mediterranean Garden. The raised beds show bold contrasts of form and colour provided by plants including silver-leaved santolinas, artemisias, and variegated and purple-leaved sages. A Mount Etna broom with a fountain of tiny yellow, deliciously scented pea flowers dominates shrub planting of cistus, buddleia and many other species.

Leaving the warm Mediterranean Garden, there is a transformation in the cool grass beneath the tall oaks, where a winding path meanders its way between lush shade-loving plants such as ferns, hostas, spotted pulmonarias and the elegant Solomon's seal, underplanted by delicate, purple-leaved violets.

Below, in a series of four pools surrounded by bog gardens, are some tall plants –

angelicas, rodgersias, irises, the umbrella plant and bright yellow trollius. Bog arums and giant gunneras contrast with candelabra primulas, water forget-me-not and *Pontederia cordata*, while, further away but still enjoying the damp conditions, astilbes are underplanted with hostas. Where the pools narrow to a canal, bushes of *Viburnum plicatum* 'Mariesii' are loaded with white flowers in spring, while irises, ferns and New Zealand flax flourish in company with marsh marigolds, senecios and pink polygonum.

Left: The fan-shaped heads of *Allium cristophii* tower above *Helianthemum* 'Rhodanthe Carneum'

Right: Like candles by the water, *Lysichiton americanus*

Below: Moisture-loving plants at the pond's edge: *Primula japonica* and *Iris laevigata* 'Alba'

BORDE HILL GARDEN West Sussex RH16 1XP

1½ miles (2.5km) north of Haywards Heath | Open daily end Mar to mid-Sep and in late Oct | Tel: 01444 450326 | **www.bordehill.co.uk**

Borde Hill is the quintessentially English country estate, comprising as it does a 16th-century mansion surrounded by both formal and intimate gardens, enveloped in turn by no less than 200 acres (81ha) of rolling Grade I*-listed parkland.

From one viewpoint, perhaps the most romantic and memorable, the mellow stone mansion appears to rise mistily from a dense cloud of blowsy, petally roses in soft shades of pink, yellow and apricot. From another it is seen, majestically, through a pair of impressive wrought-iron gates.

The property was purchased in the late 19th century by Colonel Stephenson Robert Clarke who created the South Lawn and installed the ha-ha. A decade later, with the family sponsoring major plant-collecting expeditions to China, the Himalayas, Burma, Tasmania, North America and the Andes, one of the main characteristics of the garden was established: that of a showplace for rare and unusual species from around the world. In 1965 Borde Hill became a registered charity

and the gardens and parkland were opened to the public for the first time.

There is such diversity packed into the 17 acres (7ha) of gardens that the visitor is spoilt for choice. Take Jay Robin's Rose Garden, designed by RHS gold medallist Robin Williams and planted in 1996. Here are some 100 varieties of David Austin roses in formal beds enclosed by low box hedges. The geometry is softened by curving paths and the roses complemented by cottage-garden plantings of peonies, phlox and delphiniums. A fountain is ringed by lavender-coloured *Nepeta faassenii* and the effect is nostalgic.

Or take the Long or Paradise Walk, the path around the boundary, to the Italian Garden accessed now by a new Camellia Walk on the east side. Where once there was a tennis court there is now a formal pool. A fountain plays in the centre, waterlilies and the reflections of surrounding trees grace the surface of the water and standard bays in pots stand guard at the corners.

The Lower Terrace has year-round interest from clouds of ornamental cherry blossom and bulbs in spring, through narrow borders massed with summer flowers – terracotta pots of geraniums and agapanthus, too – and on to the changing hues of trees and shrubs in autumn. Parterres edged with golden box and planted with pittosporum, santolina and salvia emphasise the Italian influence.

By contrast, cool shades and subtle colours characterise the planting on the Upper Terrace where geometric beds are edged with myrtle. There is a horticultural

project in progress here: fine examples of *Magnolia grandiflora* 'Kay Parris', which has fragrant, creamy-white flowers in July, are being trained as standards.

On to the Long Dell, where many fine trees were tragically destroyed in the gales of 1987. This area has now been given an intensely Sino-Himalayan theme; shades of those early expedition plantings. Hardy Chusan palms (*Trachycarpus fortunei*), the principal survivors of the 1987 storm, now form the foundation of the planting in this former stone quarry where there are many rare and interesting botanical species, some of which were donated by the Royal Botanic Gardens at Kew.

Noteworthy specimens include the dogwood *Cornus controversa*, the early-spring-flowering *Osmanthus yunnanensis* and paulownia species with their foxglove-like flowers. In spring the north side of the Dell is all shades of pink, yellow, orange and blue when the azaleas are in bloom and the ground is carpeted with bluebells.

Further glorious azalea specimens lay the foundation of the Azalea Ring, where the centrepiece is *Cornus kousa* and other plantings include *Magnolia x soulangeana* 'Brozzonii' and *Emmenopterys henryi*.

All of these form but a small part of the Borde Hill collection of trees and shrubs, said to be one of the finest in the country. So, too,

is the collection of champion trees, granted that status because of their outstanding height and/or girth. Among 80 of these world-beaters are *Discaria discolor, Fraxinus nigra* and *Chamaecyparis lawsoniana* 'Wareana' to name just a few.

More trees of champion-like proportions are shown to spectacular effect in the Garden of Allah. This area, originally part of the parkland, was cultivated in the 1920s with rhododendrons collected by Frank Kingdon-Ward and later so-named because of its aura of peace and tranquillity.

A visit to the Old Potting Sheds is to look back in time, to the days when there were 26 full-time gardeners at Borde Hill; fruit, vegetables and flowers were produced for the house and myriad plants grown from seed and propagated from cuttings. Now a remaining wall shelters tender and unusual species, mainly from South Africa and South America, and a small enclosure has a trough planted with *Corokia virgata* whose yellow flowers are followed by bright orange fruits, and *Sollya heterophylla*, both originating from New Zealand.

Borde Hill, a garden, woodland and parkland of such variety, has so much to offer to plant-lovers and, in keeping with its earlier objective, is still showcasing plants from around the globe.

Left: With a look of such intense concentration, the child statue could be tending the patch of irises!

Below: The Rose Garden at Borde Hill with its pathway leading up to a delightful circular pond surrounded by *Nepeta faassenii*

Right: With their densely clustered rose-pink blooms, rhododendrons in the West Garden form the prettiest of archways

BROUGHTON CASTLE Oxfordshire OX15 5EB

 3 miles (5km) south west of Banbury | **Open selected days Easter to mid-Sep** | **Tel: 01295 276070** | **www.broughtoncastle.com**

Standing in the lush Oxfordshire countryside, Broughton Castle is a castellated manor house, dating from 1300 and greatly enlarged in the middle of the 16th century. Its intimate 3-acre (1ha) garden is surrounded by a large moat. In 1900 there were no fewer than 14 gardeners at Broughton, but Lord and Lady Saye have simplified the structure while preserving the grandeur of the setting. The late Lanning Roper suggested opening up the views across the park, and the garden now consists of four magnificent borders and an enclosed, formal parterre.

Backed by a 14th-century stone wall, the Battlement Border has a colour scheme of blue and yellow, white and grey. Here, the main shrub roses are 'Maigold', a vigorous climber with semi-double bronze-yellow blooms, 'Golden Wings', the fragrant, apricot-coloured 'Buff Beauty', and 'Windrush'. The west-facing border also holds *Campanula lactiflora*, willowherb, the creamy-white flowers of *Philadelphus* 'Manteau d'Hermine' and hypericum. The other long border concentrates its colours on blues, pinks and reds, with *Rosa* 'Fantin-Latour', *R. rubrifolia*

and *R.* 'Fritz Nobis' set against potentillas, eupatorium, philadelphus and *Clematis* 'Broughton Star'.

The enclosed formal layout is the square Ladies' Garden. Borders flank walls which are all that remain of the 16th-century kitchens, the mullioned windows bearing testimony to the original purpose of the building. Laid out originally about a century ago, there are four fleur-de-lys beds surrounded by miniature box hedges which contain *Rosa* 'Gruss an Aachen' and *R.* 'Lavender Lassie', and two circular beds of lavender.

Against the castle wall is a fine display of the double pale-pink flowers of *Rosa* 'Felicia', and there are mixed borders on both sides of this enclosure. Everywhere at Broughton is a profusion of old-fashioned roses and sweeping flows of colour. The harmony that has been achieved between the serenity of the castle itself and the beauty of its garden setting adds greatly to the pleasure of a visit to this most English of castles.

Left: Mirror image: the magnificent 14th-century manor house and neighbouring church reflected in the moat

Right: The height of summer with scents of lavender and roses and a romantic blend of pretty pastel shades

Below: Formal planting in the square Ladies' Garden

CHENIES MANOR
Buckinghamshire WD3 6ER

1 mile (1.5km) north of Little Chalfont | Open selected days | Tel: 01494 762888 | **www.cheniesmanorhouse.co.uk**

Chenies Manor has a long and noble history and has been graced by visits from two English monarchs. The magnificent brick manor house was built in 1460 for Sir John Cheyne and enlarged in 1526 by Sir John Russell, later to become the first Earl of Bedford. The gardens that so exquisitely complement the Tudor house are the design and creation of the present owner, Elizabeth MacLeod Matthews. Each one of the garden compartments – the Rose Garden, the Sunken Garden and the South Border among them – displays her brilliantly artistic use of colour and texture. She uses permanent plantings of shrubs and foliage plants as a year-round canvas against which to ring the plant changes season by season.

Tulips are Elizabeth MacLeod Matthews' speciality and in the Chenies Manor garden she has shown how versatile, elegant yet flamboyant they can be. The peak of the spring season is when some 7,000 tulips are composed throughout the gardens in impact-making blocks of single colours. The White Garden sparkles with only white and the palest yellow. The colours strengthen considerably to buttercup yellow and red through orange in the South Border and, in the Rose Garden close to the house, pinks and mauves paint a romantically pretty picture. It is left to the Sunken Garden to illustrate the plant's flamboyance; there they are displayed in a mixed colour palette. And wherever there are tulips there is an understorey of, as appropriate, pink and white bellis daisies, pale and deep blue forget-me-nots and many-hued wallflowers.

Before the fiesta of tulips, the gardens come alive in a number of ways. A 150-foot (45-metre) arched walkway is bordered by narcissi and many-coloured hellebores to be followed by the stately globes of mauve and white alliums. The arches are wreathed in sweetly scented *Clematis armandii*. At a time when the tender greenhouse-grown perennials are ready to be planted out, late spring beds and borders put on a gentle blue, mauve and pink cloak, some speckled with blue and white campanulas, iris and sisyrinchium blended with intensely pretty lime-green lady's mantle (*Alchemilla mollis*).

In summer the gardens take on, variously, the appearance of a brilliantly sunny day and one casting dappled shade. The bright-blue-sky ambience is matched with dahlias in pinks and reds mixed with purple petunias, blue salvias and the ermine-crimson *Lobelia cardinalis*. Self-sown *Eryngium* 'Miss Willmott's Ghost' serves to dilute and separate the jazzy colours.

By contrast, the Rose Garden casts a romantic spell. Surely Henry VIII, who stayed here with his bride, Catherine Howard, would have delighted to wander here. There are many historic roses, some with a lineage almost as old as the manor house itself: Bourbon and musk roses, hybrid perpetuals and repeat-flowering English roses. Between-planting of pink, white and mauve cosmos casts a delightful veil over the rose beds, whilst towering onopordum thistles make a strong architectural statement.

The Physic Garden, too, has its roots in medieval times. Planted around a centuries-old wall, there are apothecary roses and hundreds of plants grouped according to their medicinal and other uses, as they would have been in monastery gardens. There are groups of plants for dyeing – such as woad, elecampane, camomile and alkanet – for antiseptic use and for perfumes, and other plants that, as in Shakespeare's time, were used to make poisons.

'Queen Elizabeth's oak tree', a favourite resting place of the monarch when she and her court stayed at the manor, commands pride of place in the parterre where a yew maze is based on an intriguing pattern of interlocking icosahedrons (20-sided figures). Dramatic bands of *Nepeta* 'Six Hills Giant' (catmint) border a path leading to the orchard, the Cutting Garden and the Kitchen Garden, which has a maze too – a penitential turf maze. Laid out in a formal potager style, this 'edible' garden is as productive as ever – perhaps due to a hard-working scarecrow.

Left: Dahlias in the Sunken Garden

Below: Tulip display in the Sunken Garden

CREUX BAILLOT COTTAGE Jersey JE3 2FE

7 miles (11.25km) north west of St Helier | Open selected days May to Sep | Tel: 01534 482191 | **www.judithqueree.com**

Left: The cottage nestles among densely planted shrubs and perennials

Right: One of the owner's collection of arisaemas, with striped spathe and giant leaves

Far right: Transport of delight in the Bog Garden!

This is a great little garden. It would be easy to be lost here; lost in admiration, that is, that Judith and Nigel Quérée have packed so much colour, interest and originality into their quarter-acre Jersey-island plot. Approaching the 300-year-old, ivy-round-the-door granite cottage along a narrow country lane – the only access – gives no hint of the dedicated and informed planting that comprises a woodland, a bog area and a dry garden; nor of the unaccountable sense of space.

Judith Quérée is a plant collector. She has collected over 200 clematis, her favourite plants; but even that is not enough. There are many more, she says, still to find. It seems that almost every structure is host to these spectacular flowers in shades from sea-foam white through sky blue, pink, lavender and magenta to deepest purple, and Judith is

proud that on every day of the year there is likely to be at least one clematis in flower. It is high-rise gardening on a glorious scale.

In the Bog Garden, kept constantly moist by natural springs even in the driest of summers, there are over 160 moisture-loving irises – another of Judith's collections.

This enthralling display includes the dramatic beardless Japanese flag, *Iris ensata*; the Siberian flag, *I. sibirica* 'Lady Vanessa', another beardless form displaying the richest of deep-purple petals blotched with lavender and flashed with white; and the hybrid *I*. 'Hatsuho,' its spectacular creamy-white, curled-back petals gilded with golden half-moons.

Nigel Quérée constructed a long, curving, planked boardwalk through the Bog Garden. Not much more than 18 inches (45cm) off

the ground and with sturdy manila rope supports, it nevertheless introduces a spirit of adventure, of discovery, and allows the plants beneath the walk to grow unhindered, as they would be by a path. In late spring this area, which seems illogically remote from other parts of the garden, is vibrant with some 35 pink, golden and orange candle primulas. Almost concurrently the 'clouds' settle, in this context clouds of minute snowy-white umbels of *Anthriscus sylvestris*, variously known as wild chervil and cow parsley, which contrast strikingly with the sword-like iris leaves.

At other times there is split-level interest, the long spikes of purple loosestrife towering above terrestrial orchids, ornamental grasses and dense, lush foliage plants. Still later, a sunshine-yellow carpet of rudbeckias appears to switch on the garden lights.

The woodland area of this Channel Island garden has yet another ambience, uniting species from China, Japan and North America. Familiar garden plants such as the sky-blue 'Bill Wallace' geranium, the mauvy-white *Primula sieboldii* and the lesser known blue-flowered *Omphalodes cappadocica* 'Cherry Ingram' have unusual neighbours – Judith's collection of around 40 arisaema plants. These tuberous perennials with their large, weird-looking, hooded spathes, some speckled, some blotched, some dramatically striped, are outstanding feature plants which have fleshy red fruits in autumn. Growing among this collection are herb Paris, *Paris polyphylla*, a summer-flowering rhizome, and

Podophyllum peltatum, which has brown-mottled light green leaves and white, cup-shaped flowers in spring.

In the Dry Garden where geraniums and sun-loving salvias – including many tender species from Central America – flourish, there is a sculpture of a young girl, The Dreamer, by Kate Denton, affectionately nicknamed Dilly Day-Dream by the Quérées. Two wire sculptures, a rooster and hen by Rupert Till, perch on the Welsh slate roof of the cottage, and two scarecrows recreate a delightful rural encounter at one of the garden fences. A life-sized figure of a gardener clutching a bundle of straw looks completely at ease leaning on the fence, while his scarecrow wife, dressed in a frock and pinny and with arms akimbo, is clearly encouraging him to return to his task.

For the last four years Judith and Nigel Quérée have been managing three meadows around their property using, as they do in their garden, totally organic principles. Their stewardship is paying dividends. They have revived an old cider apple tree, increased the biodiversity of the land and reduced the noxious weeds that had taken hold. But here, as in the garden, as always, Judith says, there is much work to be done.

One of the most notable of Judith's collections is the unusual and curiously shaped arisaema plants which seem to flourish so dramatically in her Bog Garden. Among them are *A. nepenthoides* which has speckled spathes, and *A. concinnum* and *A. ciliatum*, both of which have striped spathes.

The plants are tuberous perennials which do best in moist but well-drained soil that is rich in humus. They like sun or partial shade and are fully to half-hardy. For best results, Judith suggests planting tubers 6 inches (15cm) deep in spring and propagating by pulling off and setting the off-sets in spring, or by planting seed. Many of the plants produce spikes of fleshy red fruits in autumn and have beautiful umbrella-like leaves.

Judith Quérée takes her gardening skills way beyond the boundaries of her own property. At the RHS Hampton Court Palace Flower Show in 2002 she won a Bronze Medal for her garden 'A Fisherman's Cottage'. With its lavender-edged shingle path and box of Jersey Royal potatoes and other vegetables displayed as if for sale on the wall, it was, Judith says, a faithful representation of a cottage at L'Etacq, St Ouen, close to Creux Baillot.

Judith enjoyed another success at a BBC TV Gardener of the Year event in Harrogate, Yorkshire, coming second in the competition with her 'Fish Out of Water' creation. Having lived most of her life within walking distance of the sea and therefore understanding how plants struggle to survive in such conditions, Judith chose to create a shingle garden with gentle contours, as if the shingle had been sculpted by the tide, and with driftwood and glass washed up as the flotsam.

DENMANS GARDEN West Sussex BN18 0SU

 7 miles (11.25km) east of Chichester | **Open daily all year, times vary; groups by appointment** | **Tel: 01243 542808** | **www.denmans-garden.co.uk**

Nestling below the South Downs is the beautiful 3½ acre (1.5ha) garden of Denmans. Like most distinguished gardens, it is continually evolving and repays regular visits by both plant-lovers and those interested in garden design because, since 1985, it has been managed and is now jointly owned by the landscape designer and author John Brookes, MBE, and Michael Neve, who has been responsible for developing Denmans into a renowned visitor attraction.

Much of the concept of the present gardens, and many of the trees that form its structure, are due to the vision of Joyce Robinson who, with her husband, bought the property in 1946. She designed the garden to have as little soil as possible showing, amassing both native and introduced trees and shrubs and – innovative at that time – using gravel extensively so that one could walk between plantings rather than past them. Mrs JHR, as she was known, died in 1996.

One of the highlights of Denmans is the Walled Garden which, sheltered by old flint walls, displays a profusion of old-fashioned roses, herbs, perennials and foliage plants – most chosen for their leaf colour – where individual plantings are allowed to self-seed at random in charming cottage-garden disarray. John Brookes' aim has been to design a garden that can translate in part to the smallest site; this is no better exemplified than in the Walled Garden which is divided into separate compartments – rooms – any one of which could be replicated in a small cottage or town garden.

South of the Walled Garden an open, grassed area divides two contrasting plantings: a hot, sunny corner and a long-since-dry gravel stream which runs down to a natural pool and is filled with plants that might once have flourished there. Seedlings are allowed to overwinter in the dry base – no damp soil to rot their roots – and are then thinned out and transplanted to grow in wild-looking mature groups.

A large pool at the bottom of the garden is framed by a seemingly random planting of water-loving species. Here, grass is cut to different lengths to accommodate spring bulbs and wild flowers. This two-height, two-tone effect is particularly striking and is a further idea that other gardeners could readily adapt.

Many of the trees planted by Mrs JHR have now matured and what was a 'hot' herbaceous corner has become a shady one, planted now with grey-leaved hostas and purple ligularia. Beyond this bed are more naturalised bulbs including winter aconites and snowdrops, crocus, narcissi and tulips. These give way to aquilegia in late spring, then to white campanulas and later to blue *Ceratostigma*. Winter in this area belongs to hellebores and the native *Iris foetidissima*.

A short walk to the Top Lawn is enhanced by a planting of Californian tree poppies (*Romneya coulteri*) and shrub roses to one side, and the lawn itself is dominated by a magnificent dawn redwood tree (*Metasequoia*). Tender species around a circular pond include *Acer palmatum* 'Senkaki' and a rare myrtle, *Myrtus apiculata*. The unheated conservatory displays a selection of succulents, some rare foliage plants and an aviary. Sculptures around the garden are by Marion Smith.

Left: The statue of a boy seated cross-legged by the pond has immense charm

Right: Complementary colours of verbascum and *Alchemilla mollis*

GREAT COMP

Kent TN15 8QS

3 miles (5km) south of Addington | Open daily Apr to Oct | Tel: 01732 885094 | **www.greatcompgarden.co.uk**

Sited in the beautiful wooded countryside of the Weald of Kent, Great Comp garden surrounds a 17th-century manor house. It was designed and created by Mr and Mrs Roderick Cameron who bought the property for their retirement in 1957 and gradually added further land so that today the garden covers 7 acres (3ha).

It is now owned by The Great Comp Charitable Trust and run by the Curator, William Dyson, assisted by a team of four gardeners and volunteers.

The great storms of 1987 and 1990 caused considerable devastation, but Great Comp remains a successful example of a plantsman's garden, with over 3,000 plants including many beautiful and rare shrubs – there are no fewer than 30 varieties of magnolia – perennials and hardy and half-hardy plants. The garden is also home to Dyson's Nurseries and their extensive collection of salvias, which is constantly being extended, both by the acquisition of new plants and by William Dyson's own breeding programme. The nursery now offers a mail order service.

This is a garden of artfully conceived surprises, the curving paths coaxing the visitor around successive bends to the next artistic and colourful plantings and eventually, almost imperceptibly, beyond the cultivated area and into wilder woodland richly planted with azaleas and rhododendrons. There, wildly overgrown faux ruins give the impression that this area has lain untended for decades; it has not, of course, but the impression persists that one is exploring an ancient site. There is a tower, and many almost-concealed ornaments; there are crumbled walls and steep stone steps with, at the top, a wooden bench; pause here for reflection. There is much to reflect upon.

Back to the artistry of the planting: close to the house, on the south side, there is a wide sweep of lawn, an area of calm broken by island beds and framed by tall, slender conifers, oaks, maples and willows skilfully underplanted with a medley of herbaceous plants – achillea, kniphofia, salvias, geum and many more.

Shape is carefully managed throughout the garden. Clipped topiary hummocks and mounds contrast engagingly with plants that are allowed to ramble and drape around and over them. An almost circular brick arch at the end of a long hedge-framed walk – one of the few straight lines in the garden – serves as a window on the lawn and borders beyond: another 'come-hither' enticement to the visitor. A brick and flint arch leads into the walled Italian Garden, created in 1994, where there are graceful urns and a pond that, surrounded by a dense planting of cordylines, is highlighted by a central pineapple fountain.

There is not a single dull moment in this garden, which was planned by two passionate plant-lovers for their retirement and is now a legacy for all to enjoy.

From the first brilliant carpeting of snowdrops and many-coloured hellebores through the fiery tones of summer's crocosmias, heleniums and dahlias, to autumn when asters, nerines and cotinus steal the show, there is interest and excitement at every turn.

Left: *Camellia japonica* 'Adolphe Audusson' colonises a brick arch

Right: A bust on a plinth is encircled by berberis, euphorbia and magnolia

Below: The spattered pink and white flowers of *Helleborus x hybridus*

GREAT DIXTER East Sussex TN31 6PH

🌼 **7 miles (11km) north west of Rye** | **Open selected days Apr to Oct** | **Tel: 01797 252878** | **www.greatdixter.co.uk**

The name of Great Dixter will be familiar to all who have read the late Christopher Lloyd's regular contributions on gardening in *Country Life* magazine and his many books, but the lively inventiveness of his horticultural style – which lives on still – nonetheless comes as a surprise, however often you visit the garden. The medieval manor was bought by Nathaniel Lloyd in 1910, and Sir Edwin Lutyens was commissioned to design the gardens; the steps and terraces that still provide the framework of the layout are distinctly his. The Sunk Garden, the topiary and the yew and box hedging were the responsibility of the owner, while his wife,

Daisy, created the wild Moat Garden and continued to help develop the garden in conjunction with her son, Christopher, after her husband's death.

The gardens at Dixter totally surround the 15th-century manor house. The lane from Northiam brings you to the north side, a flagstone path leading straight through a lovely meadow area to the medieval porch. In summer yellow and orange lilies grow in pots to brighten the timber-framed façade, while ferns flourish beneath the windows and the lawn supports a Chilean bamboo and an old common pear. Nearby, on this north side, is the colourful Sunk Garden with an octagonal

pool surrounded by drystone walls, the enclosure framed by barn walls and a yew hedge. Ferns and Kenilworth ivy grow out of crevices in the paving, and geraniums and lavender support the rich border planting of campanulas, astrantias, *Eryngium giganteum*, variegated euonymus, day lilies and lychnis.

In the Walled Garden, spare a glance for the *Clematis x jouiniana* 'Praecox', and for the blue thistles, euphorbias and mallows, before leaving via a flight of steps characteristic of Lutyens' style. Continue past a bed of hydrangeas, rodgersias and geraniums to the topiary lawn, inhabited by great topiary birds and abstract shapes in clipped yew. The old moat is seeded with grasses and is bright in spring with moon daisies, knapweed and clover, while a splendid magnolia makes a dramatic seasonal show.

The Long Border is strong in colour contrasts, with golden elder and Mount Etna broom set against white hydrangeas, variegated golden hostas and mahonia. Sea hollies make a regular appearance, while the blue of *Campanula lactiflora*, *Euonymus* 'Silver Queen' and pink diascias contribute to a rich display. The golden shower of *Ulmus* 'Dicksonii' attracts the eye in the middle of the border with silver-grey willows underplanted with blue veronica and purple everlasting peas.

Left: Great Dixter in winter with frosted teasels in the foreground

Right: Colourful plants growing cottage-garden style in front of the house

Below: *Dahlia* **'David Howard' with** *Canna* **'Wyoming' in the Exotic Garden**

HADDON LAKE HOUSE Isle of Wight PO38 1XR

2½ miles (4km) south west of Ventnor | Guided tours only, by prior appointment | Tel: 01983 855151 | www.lakehousedesign.co.uk

On the southernmost tip of the Isle of Wight, nestling into the Undercliff at St Lawrence, is the newly restored garden at Haddon Lake House, a perfect marriage of contrasting styles, each within its own space. Formerly part of the pleasure grounds of a gracious Victorian marine residence, the site had been split away from the house many years ago and become overgrown and desolate. The former *pièce de résistance* of the property, the lake, had also been totally neglected and was dark and dank. A daunting prospect!

Here, landscape designer Phillippa and Steve Lambert, an architectural illustrator, self-built their house in the style of a Japanese boat-house, with decking extending

Above: A herringbone-pattern brick pathway with repeat plantings of *Aster x frikartii* 'Monch' and *Euphorbia ceratocarpa* leads up to a greenhouse with low hedge, conical-shaped bay trees and a rose arbour in the foreground

Left: Dark burgundy *Dahlia* 'Karma Naomi'

Right: Arctotis, rudbeckia, *Salvia farinacea* 'Victoria' and *Cosmos bipinnatus* 'Pink Bonbon'

over the now-revitalised lake. Planning permission to build the house was granted only on the condition that they restored the landscape; in only two years from 2002 they had in fact revitalised the whole property.

A gravelled path frames the lake, now with a sparkling, gravity-fed fountain and cascades – the perceived 'front garden' of the house. Behind the property, backed by a border with sub-tropical planting, there is a minimalist, Japanese-style courtyard, a cool, elegant design with neutral and grey decorative paving, subdued foliage planting and contemporary seating.

In a completely contrasting genre the Victorian Kitchen Garden, another victim of neglect, has been brought back to life and abundant productivity with a cornucopia of fruits, vegetables and herbs grown alongside a kaleidoscopic mix of annual flowers. Self-sufficiency is the keynote of the walled garden, as it would have been in Victorian times, and most plants, grown organically, are raised from seed or propagated from cuttings.

Topiary arches, pyramids and domes give architectural form and herringbone brick and resin-bonded pathways set the scene with an air of orderliness and formality. At opposite ends of the garden there are rectangular raised beds stocked with a profusion of strawberries and blueberries, runner beans and sweetcorn, together with colourful cottage-garden favourites including the lavender-coloured *Salvia farinacea* 'Victoria', clumps of purple and white cosmos and stately magenta gladioli.

The route to the restored Victorian greenhouse and potting shed is enhanced by a profusion of herbs almost colonising the paths and by near-primary-coloured borders with repeat plantings of vibrant red and

yellow rudbeckias and dahlias, the yellow-green *Salvia officinalis* 'Icterina', *Ageratum* 'Blue Bouquet' and the graceful purple *Verbena bonariensis*.

The advantageous micro-climate of this south-coastal region made it possible for the Lamberts to recreate the woodland with semi-exotic trees and plants. Now, a world away from their natural *milieu*, there is a

wide diversity of species including olives, gingers, agaves and massive tree ferns; another area, another significant restoration; another contrasting habitat in this garden of surprises.

Understandably perhaps, the restoration and rejuvenation project of the Haddon Lake gardens that Phillippa and Steve Lambert have achieved, and in such a remarkably

short time, has been likened to that of a miniature Lost Gardens of Heligan in a marine setting. Both gardens are most definitely 'see-worthy'.

87

HATFIELD HOUSE

1 mile (1.5km) south east of Hatfield | Open selected days from late Mar to Oct | Tel: 01707 287010 | www.hatfield-house.co.uk

Both setting and history combine to make the gardens of Hatfield House one of the most outstanding in the country. The Jacobean house was built between 1607 and 1611 by Robert Cecil, chief minister to King James II, and this mellow brick building, together with the remaining great hall wing of the Old Palace of Hatfield, where Princess Elizabeth was confined during her sister Mary's reign, provide the backdrop for

gardens that were originally planted by John Tradescant the Elder. Today, the gardens are maintained and developed by the present Marchioness, Lady Salisbury, and her small team of gardeners.

From Palace Green you pass directly into the West Garden and to a stunning blue and silver border which has recently been replanted. Steps up to the Lime Walk enable the visitor to look down onto the Old Palace

Knot Garden in the manner in which it might have been seen in the 17th century. The knot hedges themselves are of box with small cones at the corners, and are filled with spring bulbs that are succeeded by flowering plants and shrubs. Crown imperials, tulips, anemones and violets bloom here in the spring, while in summer shrub roses contrast in shape and colour with delphiniums and pinks.

Yew hedges border the Privy Garden, and there is a pleached Lime Walk on all four sides. In springtime the beds are filled with euphorbias, alliums and hellebores. Later, peonies and mauve and red penstemons come into flower, and shrub roses give height to the planting.

A beautiful Longitude Dial was installed as a central feature in the West Garden as part of the 400th anniversary celebrations – including concerts, exhibitions and firework displays – that took place throughout 2011. The Dial is surrounded by scented plants and shrubs, including the beautiful pink rose named 'Lady Salisbury' especially for the anniversary year.

A gate leads you into the Woodland Garden, a wilderness, with paths through a wild flower meadow. In spring this wonderful area is bright with rhododendrons, camellias and magnolias underplanted with crocuses and hellebores.

One day in each week (check the website for details) visitors can enjoy the tranquillity of the East Garden at the front of the house, which was laid out by the fifth Marquess of Salisbury and designed to be viewed from the first floor of the house. The formal box beds are planted with a diversity of unusual plants, and there is a spectacular parterre, a lake and an orchard. Entry is through the vegetable garden.

Hatfield House gardens combine historical layout with modern plantsmanship of the very highest standard. The West Garden is frequently used for exhibitions of contemporary sculpture and special events.

LITTLE LODGE GARDEN
Surrey KT7 0BX

🌼 **2 miles (3.2km) south west of Kingston-upon-Thames | Open selected days by appointment | Tel: 020 8339 0931**

The approach to Little Lodge is intriguing. It is as if the house is the background scenery for a stage set. Season by season, it is thickly curtained in the pale green leaves of wisteria and then with cascades of the mauve flowers. The narrow border along the front of the house – the stage – is defined with a low box hedge grown by the owners from cuttings. But this is no ordinary hedge. It has dips and rises, like an exquisitely draped garland, and is unusually attractive. Set behind the hedge are the stars of the show, standard bay trees and pots of

clipped box topiaries, each decorated with a perching topiary bird.

Opposite the house, where once there was an air-raid shelter and then a rock garden, there is now a wildlife pond packed with moisture-loving plants and adding an extra dimension to this third-of-an-acre garden.

Julia and Peter Hickman bought the property 40 years ago, and he insists that the garden 'really did just happen'. His plan has always been to concentrate on plants that do well in the summer, there in South East

England, and on soft colours. 'Nothing too garish', he said with feeling. Gradually over time, areas of lawn have given way to richly planted herbaceous borders and features have been added – a secret garden, pergolas and arches, a productive vegetable garden and a great many containerised plants 'to fill the terrace and paths'.

An archway in a yew hedge (formed over a hazel twig support) leads to a secret garden, at its best in early summer. A stone cherub bird bath in a circular bed rises from a thick carpet of lily-of-the-valley

and, creating a luxuriantly verdant group, there are hellebores and Solomon's seal (*Polygonatum*). Tall purple and white spires of goat's rue, *Galega* 'His Majesty', look stately beside a large, hummocky bush of white tree poppy. A thick, enveloping canopy of yellowy-green ivy, *Hedera algeriensis* 'Marginomaculata', covers an arch around a shady water feature where ferns flourish. Completing the cameo there are the delicate pansy flowers of *Viola x wittrockiana* 'Silver Princess', lime-green nicotiana, and grouped terracotta pots of rock, alpine and succulent plants.

More and more areas of the brick terrace at the back of the house disappear as containers of mainly succulents are added. Stone shapes cut from lumps of solid rock from the Isle of Purbeck and made into garden sinks, alongside terracotta pots and dishes, compose an eclectic group. They display the bright-green glossy rosettes of *Aeonium arboreum* 'Zwartkop', the dark-green, red-tinted rosettes of *Sempervivum grandiflorum*, the aubergine-coloured leaves of *S. tectorum*, and *Aegopodium podagraria* 'Variegatum', bishop's weed. Dainty pink viola flowers dangling over the group provide charming texture contrast. Other planters close to the house display dwarf acers and dwarf conifers and large standard hollies that the Hickmans grew and shaped themselves.

Borders in an informal, partly walled garden and edging a lawn are richly stocked with shrubs and herbaceous plants, creating the tranquil atmosphere that is Julia Hickman's stated aim. They also capture the essence of summer. In one border, the plant associations – almost all in her husband's declared preference for subtle shades – include field poppies (*Papaver rhoeas*) and the bushy tree poppy, *Romneya coulteri*, lavishly spattered with fragrant white flowers, mingling with tall white spires of

Verbascum chaixii, and dusky pink valerian, *Centranthus ruber*.

Elsewhere there is an inspired partnership as tall, elegant, yellowy-green globes of angelica provide background height and interest against clusters of mauve and white *Campanula persicifolia*, white *Salvia officinalis* and *Lathyrus grandiflorus*, everlasting pea, which so delightfully twines around anything and everything in its path. Peter says he does his best to 'casual train' it and does sometimes succeed. The cheerful welcome he gives to self-sown annuals does mean that plants 'pop up all over the place' in a charmingly naturalistic way.

In a garden that especially celebrates summer, roses have an understandably important role to play. Long thick ribbons of the 1917 species rambler *Rosa mulliganii* (formerly *R. longicuspis*) eventually overcame an old apple tree and now entwine a pear tree that was grown from a cutting. The white flowers have an unusual banana-like scent. The hybrid musk rose 'Buff Beauty', with large trusses of fragrant apricot-yellow flowers, and the sweetly scented pink blooms of 'Felicia' blend with other flowers in the borders.

The vegetable garden is planted against a background of the delightful climbing *Rosa* 'Dortmund', its flat, single red flowers having the appearance of wild roses growing in the hedgerows. Neat rows of canes support runner beans, some vegetable beds are bordered with box hedges (not garlanded here) and there are peas, broad beans, brassicas – a profusion of crops too numerous to mention. A jokey feature in this seriously productive part of the garden is a huge terracotta sculpture of a pear; if it were real it would win first prize the world over.

Beyond the lawn there is a small area where Peter is creating a wild flower meadow. His first step was to sprinkle the seeds of yellow rattle, an annual parasite, over the grass and to place two steamer chairs among the seedheads. It looks the perfect place from which to contemplate this delightful country-style garden that belies its proximity to the metropolitan stage.

Left: The front garden with wildlife pond surrounded by damp-loving bog plants

Above: Silene, hesperis, *Allium cristophii* and *Viola cornuta*

LOSELEY PARK Surrey GU3 1HS

There is a sense of continuity about Loseley Park, which has been in the ownership of the same family for 500 years. Set in ancient Surrey parkland close to the North Downs, the house was built in 1562, in the reign of Queen Elizabeth I, by Sir William More, an ancestor of the present owner, Michael More-Molyneux.

Covering a 2½-acre (1ha) site, the Walled Garden is divided into separate 'rooms', each with its own individual planting scheme and character. The Flower Garden with its maze of pathways and rectangular island bed combines traditional herbaceous plants and shrubs planted with admirable density. Groups of burnt-orange rudbeckia,

crocosmia and kniphofia are towered over by yellow-flowering mullein, and the moody blue delphiniums and agapanthus are complemented by the purple alliums and foxgloves.

The border facing the south side of the tennis lawn has a characteristic that will be familiar to many garden-lovers: the influence of Gertrude Jekyll, a friend of the More-Molyneux family. On one of her visits to take afternoon tea at Loseley Park in the early 1900s she sketched out a scheme that lives on today. Her signature ideas for the use of progressively warm and cool colours, ranging from fiery reds and oranges through pastel tones then fading into greys and purples,

are so painterly that the border could have been designed specifically to delight a landscape artist. Contributing to this scheme there are dahlias, cotton lavender, nepeta and kniphofia, the Jekyll effect achieved by amassing many hundreds of plants.

'Cool' is the overall theme of the planting in the White Garden, where borders of white, silver and cream surround a central fountain and pool. Lacecap hydrangeas, eryngium and grasses give structure to the borders, together with *Agastache* 'Liquorice White' (Mexican giant hyssop), *Euphorbia* 'Diamond Frost' and osteospermums. Varieties of cosmos that sparkle in this setting include 'Purity', 'Pied Piper' and 'Blush White'.

Low box hedges frame beds of old English roses – over 1,000 bushes in all – in the Rose Garden, at its peak from mid-June to early July when the colour palette is captivating and the scent heady. A series of rose-covered arbours and pyramidal wigwams showcase climbers and ramblers.

There are over 200 culinary, medicinal, household and decorative herbs in the Herb Garden – as many, surely, as there were in the days when the kitchen gardens supplied the household. With interest in herbs growing all the time, the staff at Loseley Park have produced a booklet to explain the *raison d'être* for many of the plantings. This is an attractive area of the garden, the mainly green, purple and yellow forms of the herbs complemented by clusters of red, pink and white hollyhocks, and their often wayward habits contrasted by mounds of clipped box.

Productivity is the keynote in the Organic Vegetable Garden where companion planting is exercised to assist in the control of pests. Amongst the beds of brassicas and leeks, root vegetables and squashes separated by wide grass paths there are sunflowers and rudbeckias and, at ground level, baskets of golden marjoram, a tapestry of fragrance and colour that would be a charming addition to any garden, anywhere.

Left: The 16th-century house rises beyond a painterly herbaceous border

Below: Rhapsody in purple: the giant mopheads of tall, stately alliums

THE MANOR HOUSE

Buckinghamshire HP27 9PD

3 miles (5km) south west of Princes Risborough | Open by appointment; see text | Tel: 01844 274292 | **www.carington.co.uk/manor-house-gardens**

Nestling deep in the Buckinghamshire countryside below the Chiltern escarpment is the Manor House at Bledlow. A serene, brick house of the early 18th century, it stands in gardens of exceptional beauty created by the owner, Lord Carrington and the late Lady Carrington, with the help of the landscape architect Robert Adams, in a style which is essentially English.

This is a garden of tremendous variety and elegance, with a mixture of formal and informal enclosures. Along the width of the house, herbaceous borders planted with roses and lavender stretch out as if to emphasise the formal structure of the building, and, beyond the immaculate lawns, a line of rectangular lily ponds shows the reds, pinks and whites of many varieties of waterlily.

Tall yew and beech hedges give a marvellous sense of enclosure for the yellow and white roses which contrast sharply with the blues and purples of lavender and heliotropium, while a sundial edged with box provides a central focus.

The formal borders, filled not only with herbaceous flowers and shrubs but also with fragrant old roses, must be seen against some equally enchanting informal areas. Here, you can sit for a while in contemplation of *Nicotiana sylvestris* towering over the bright colours of antirrhinums and fuchsias, and the stunning combination of shimmering

tufts of silver santolina interplanted with purple heliotropium.

Inside the walled kitchen garden, bright blue salvias, penstemons and peonies mingle with statuesque runner beans and other vegetables, and York stone paths lead to an enchanting, rose-covered gazebo.

A sculpture garden has recently been designed on a sloping site with wide, open views: underneath a canopy of mature trees, large modern figures playfully roll on the lawns, their white bodies contrasting with the spiky buddleia behind.

Although the gardens of the Manor House are open on only a few days in the year, by written appointment from May to September, the tranquil Lyde Garden is open to the public every day and is worth visiting at any time of year. A series of wooden paths, bridges and walkways lead through this stunning water garden where there are many unusual species of plant to be seen.

Left: Massed, all-of-a-kind planting within the curved parterres creates strong contrasts of colour and texture

Below: A walkway in the Lyde Garden where there are many unusual, moisture-loving species

7 miles (11.25km) south east of Basingstoke | Open weekdays (not BH) May, Jun and Jul | Tel: 01256 862827 | www.gertrudejekyllgarden.co.uk

In an idyllic village close to the town of Basingstoke there is one of the finest garden restorations of recent years.

When Mr and Mrs J Wallinger came to the Manor House, Upton Grey, in 1984, the gardens were almost derelict, but as a result of careful research and meticulous and determined work, the layout and planting conceived by Gertrude Jekyll between 1908 and 1909 are now fully matured and a worthy setting for the house designed by that eminent country-house architect of the Edwardian period, Ernest Newton.

To achieve such a faithful and authentic restoration Mrs Wallinger managed to obtain all 19 of Gertrude Jekyll's plans dated between 1908 and 1909 and use the majority of the species and cultivars specified in her recreation of this iconic garden. In the few cases where plants had been lost she chose close substitutes of similar dates.

Perhaps even more exciting is the recreation, to the west of the house, of the only Jekyll wild garden known to have survived. Here, shallow grass steps enter the garden, and sinuous paths wind their way between lilac and rambling roses, such as 'Jersey Beauty', 'Blush Rambler', 'Dundee Rambler' and 'The Garland', while hollies, laburnum, quince and medlar, weeping ash and walnuts give shape to the layout. In the beds leading to the pond, kniphofia and hemerocallis attract the eye. Naturalised daffodils give a strong start to the season.

Left: Paths wind down through rose and fruit trees to reach the secluded tranquillity of the pond

Right: Clusters of pale-pink peonies make a delightful display in the Rose Garden, seen here across a border 'painted' bright pink with valerian

On the other side of the house a pergola stands between lawns and two narrow borders that are planted with sedum, iris, *Anemone sylvestris*, *Asphodeline lutea* and *Penstemon glaber*. Here steps lead down to a rose garden. The retaining walls are planted with campanula, aubretia and cerastium, while the footing beds hold choisya, eryngium, rosemary and nepeta. In the beds, lilies and canna are surrounded by peonies, roses and stachys, while two further deep beds have a typically cool colour scheme provided by *Santolina incana*, acanthus, hosta, lavender and rosemary.

Above the Rose Garden, lupins, rudbeckia, delphinium and hollyhocks stand behind pale spiderwort, kniphofia and *Nepeta mussinii*. The herbaceous border on the other side of the garden contains coreopsis, spirea and senecio in front of dahlias, asters and helianthus. The colours run in drifts from pale blues and yellows at each end of the borders, rising to a climax of red with *Papaver orientale* and orange day lilies in the centre.

MILLE FLEURS Guernsey GY7 9DW

1 mile (1.5km) from St Pierre du Bois | Open by appointment | Tel: 01481 263911 | **www.millefleurs.co.uk**

Above: Sub-tropical plants luxuriate in this Channel Island environment

Right: *Brugmansia sanguinea* in the area known as the Jungle

Far right: *Rosa* 'La France' exemplifies the 'roses-round-the-door' description

The name of the traditional Guernsey farmhouse, Mille Fleurs, is defined as 'a pattern of many different colourful flowers, leaves and vines' or 'a perfume distilled from several different kinds of flower'. The garden that Jane and David Russell have created there lives up to both definitions. Their 2½-acre (1ha) garden is a blissful pot pourri of cottage-garden flowers and sub-tropical plants, many inspired by their travels to Thailand and South Africa, and all equally at home in this benevolently mild climate.

The farmhouse is settled on top of a steeply wooded conservation valley and has views across a reservoir, which attracts many different bird species, to a nature reserve beyond. When the Russells moved to the property in 1985 their first task was to clear away the thicket of uncontrolled undergrowth and expose the existing network of paths and terraces. Their second was to plant a framework

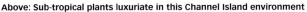

of native trees such as oak and ash to give structure to the garden and provide a habitat for birds and other wildlife. With that established, they created a garden that is in parts as romantically pretty as any cottage garden and in parts excitingly, uncharacteristically lush.

Around the farmhouse and three holiday cottages tucked away in a corner nearby, the planting is unashamedly conventional, of the roses-round-the-door kind; literally in some cases. Fragrant jasmine and honeysuckle ramble so enthusiastically over the wall of the house that the windows seem like peepholes, and climbing roses give further veracity to the 'distilled perfume' definition.

A series of paths zigzags down the side of the valley, levelling out at first one terrace and then another, each one offering a breathtaking view. At the bottom of the valley, an area the owners have dubbed the Jungle, tender and sub-tropical plants flourish in a sheltered micro-climate; palms, cannas, gingers and bananas creating a density of lush foliage. Here a 100-year-old Tasmanian xanthorrhoea (black boy or grass tree) was the main attraction until one of Jane's newest acquisitions, a blue hesper palm, replaced it and took on the starring role. In another corner of the garden, in complete contrast to this showcase of exotics, there is a bluebell and wild flower copse, a hazy sea of blue in spring and, when the foxgloves are in flower, a mixed colour-washed palette in early summer.

Three small ponds fed by natural springs are the focus for a tree fernery and bog garden inspired by a visit to the Lost Gardens of Heligan in Cornwall. Here, mature tree ferns stand tall, casting the shade of their giant umbrellas over astilbes, bog primulas, hostas, gunnera and other moisture- and shade-loving plants. Cut into a sloping,

sun-filled lawn, the South African border, too, is planted with species far from their natural *milieu*, peach-coloured watsonia, pink dierama (wandflowers), restios and protea among them, all looking perfectly at home.

In this sun-trapping area of the garden a swimming pool glistens beside a bank of dry, arid soil intensely planted with more sun-loving plants, creating a gold, orange and yellow curtain. Gazanias and crocosmia spatter the bank with colour, phormium and aloes, aeonium and agaves give form, and a large mature fig tree presides. Terracotta pots around the pool, planted with brilliant red pelargoniums, seem to turn up the heat. There is nothing random about Jane Russell's choice of colours and nowhere is there a jarring note. Colours progress seamlessly from this riot of fiery hues back through a series of colour-themed areas before

returning to the comparative calm of the plants enveloping the house.

The ground around the farmhouse was once a cider orchard and then during World War II was given over to intensive fruit and vegetable production. A part of it has reverted to the latter role. The Russells have recently extended a fruit, vegetable and cutting garden to provide produce and flowers for the house and for their self-catering guests; and, they say wryly, for the birds and rabbits.

Apart from the island's famous 'Guernsey Tom' tomatoes, which are a 'must', they experiment with less everyday crops such as melons, sweet potatoes, Thai chillies, Chinese artichokes, custard squash and borlotti beans. In the vegetable garden, as in the rest of the acreage, there is a successful marriage of the familiar and the exotic.

PENSHURST PLACE Kent TN11 8DG

5 miles (8km) south west of Tonbridge | Open weekends in Feb, selected days Mar to Oct | Tel: 01892 870307 | **www.penshurstplace.com**

Although there has been a garden at Penshurst Place, in the Weald of Kent, since the 14th century, the layout that one sees today was largely determined in the time of the first Elizabeth.

In the 1550s Sir Henry Sidney moved thousands of tons of soil to build a great parterre to the south of the house, 360 feet (110 metres) by 300 feet (91 metres), retained by walls and terraces. During the family's decline in the 18th and 19th centuries this structure was left broadly intact, and the present owner's great-grandfather, the 2nd Lord De L'Isle and Dudley, created the magnificent Italian garden on the Elizabethan parterre and planted the yew hedges which are so much a feature of Penshurst. The late Viscount De L'Isle, who came to the house in 1945, restored the gardens so that, today, they are a feast of colour set within a firm architectural framework.

On entering the gardens you are struck by the new design by Chelsea Gold Medal winner George Carter; backed by yew and overhung with apple trees. Flag irises, anemones, achillea, hemerocallis, lilies and astilbes welcome the visitor with their seasonal colour, while beyond the hedge are the Rose Garden and the Heraldic Garden. In the first, four beds of *Rosa* 'King Arthur' are edged with red berberis and *R.* 'Elizabeth of Glamis' with lavender. Among the standard roses are 'Iceberg', 'Etoile de Holland' and 'Mischief', and beneath them the velvety *Stachys lanata*. In the Heraldic Garden, rows of nut trees are underplanted with daffodils and tulips for stunning spring colour, to be followed later on by the warm colours of hardy fuchsias and spire lilies.

Left: Perfect symmetry: the central pool at the heart of the parterre

Right: A breathtakingly beautiful display of vibrant pink peonies

Between these two layouts is the Middle Walk, designed as a shrub border by the late Lanning Roper, with the bright reds and yellows of senecio, cotinus, phlomis and *Sedum spectabile*, and in the end hedge there is a 'window' matched by a squint in the house. The Italian parterre centres on an oval fountain surrounded by dwarf box hedges enclosing 'Elizabeth Arden' roses, and the terrace walls are draped with 'New Dawn' and 'Queen Elizabeth'.

The Tudor Terrace is planted with red acers, while the Nut Garden has coppiced Kentish cobnuts and four avenues of crab apples lushly underplanted with a mixture of miniature daffodils, bluebells, primroses, tulips and cowslips. An Inner Pergola, covered with wisteria, honeysuckle and climbing roses, stands romantically in the middle.

Halfway down the Yew Alley is Diana's Bath, a lily pond where water hyacinths and aponogeton flourish. To the south is the attractive Grey Garden, created by John Codrington, which is full of delicate artemisias and dianthus beneath the willow-leaved pear. The Stage Garden, once the drying ground, is covered in a variety of flowering shrubs, while, alongside, the Magnolia Garden boasts a particularly fine *Magnolia x soulangeana*.

A popular (and patriotic) feature is the Flag Garden, in which the pattern and colours of the Union Jack are represented in flowers. Red and white roses take pride of place, interspersed with with blue lavender.

PETTIFERS Oxfordshire OX17 1RU

5 miles (8km) north east of Banbury | Open by appointment; no dogs | Tel: 01295 750232 | www.pettifers.com

A well-defined garden plan sets the scene for country-style planting in a bold colour palette. As the garden sweeps gracefully down from the 17th-century farmhouse it becomes gradually less formal until, at length, it merges into the Oxfordshire countryside. This is a garden completely at ease in its setting; one which harnesses the distant views to glorious advantage.

Pettifers garden, at the home of Mr and the Honourable Mrs James Price, has taken over 18 years to create – one is tempted to write 'to perfect' – and it is evolving still. It has a ground plan of moss-covered brick paths and dry stone walls, with clipped box hedges forming parterres and defining borders. There are clipped box globes of varying sizes and both randomly spaced and rows of flat-topped yew pillars. Even these, so often marks of formality and conformity in a garden design, do not detract from the impression of originality and freedom.

It is the uninhibited use of colour and unusual plant pairings that make this garden so innovative. Gina Price attributes her freedom with plant colour to her many trips to India. It is interesting to note that bold colour pairings can so successfully cross continents. Her appreciation of the use of colour crosses national borders too. The glorious carved stable doors with their terracotta and blue criss-cross trellis pattern, taken from the castle of Würzburg in Bavaria,

make a fascinating background to a variety of plant combinations. The wrought-iron windows were inspired by the decoration of flowers on the Taj Mahal.

Below a terrace close to the house there are low retaining walls planted with alpines. At a lower level a large central lawn separates two long flower borders backed by hedges and trees. Low clipped hedges outline parterres which take on different characteristics season by season.

Planting always in groups of at least nine or eleven, Gina Price achieves the maximum impact with each plant colour. Even viewed from a distance, each plant group can be clearly identified, never merging into a faded palette.

Gradually Gina Price has been replanting some borders, replacing shrubs and perennials that have a short flowering season with grasses that change colour so effectively through summer and autumn. Most of the perennials she uses are chosen because they have a good leaf shape or long flowering season.

In one border, bronze and maroon achillea and purple Michaelmas daisies are interplanted with an explosion of golden, red and green grasses whose lively forms and varying hues will span the seasons. In a similar way, grasses enhance a patch of

terracotta achillea, purple allium, the violet-blue flowers of aconitum and the lemon-yellow evening primrose.

The purple/yellow/orange theme is repeated in autumn in a border where the golden *Crocosmia* 'Walberton Yellow' and orange and yellow *Kniphofia rooperi* mingle with daisy-like heleniums and the pinkish-purple flowers of joe pye weed, *Eupatorium purpureum* 'Riesenschirm'.

In a summer planting, where the colour influence is unmistakably Indian, purple alliums and asters and the violet-flowered *Rosa* 'Reine des Violettes' vie with scarlet poppies and the orange-red *Euphorbia* 'Fern Cottage'. A wooden bench painted in a toning shade of lilac is 'planted' among the flowers, perhaps in readiness for an artist to capture the painterly scene.

Where Gina Price has used white it is to emphasise and complement rich or strong shades in other plants. In a parterre, white agapanthus contrast so strongly with deep-maroon dahlias that, in bright sunlight, those blooms seem almost black. In a cool border planted with *Achillea* 'Coronation Gold', the golden grass *Miscanthus sinensis* 'Cabaret' and greeny-yellow euphorbia, the nearly-white regal lilies and towering spires of white delphinium seem to make their neighbours take on an even brighter shade of gold.

Each of the parterres that defines parts of the Pettifers design is like a miniature

garden within a garden. Edged by low clipped box hedges, each one contains permanent features in the shape of four tall, flat-topped cones and a cluster of stubby spheres. The implied formality of the enclosure is belied by the planting – in one, a confusion of apricot shrub roses and dahlias edged by sky-blue agapanthus, their long, arching stems forming unruly wavy lines. Another parterre has cluster planting of apricot, maroon, pink and yellow dahlias with blue glazed pots of peach-coloured single dahlias.

Edged by a brick path and a low hedge, the Cutting Garden has the nostalgic appeal of an old-fashioned cottage garden. Sweet peas clamber up both sides of a wigwam row, purple clematis covers a lone cane wigwam, and poppies ramble among clipped box shapes that can do nothing to impose an air of formality.

A wide grass path cuts through an avenue of tall, flat-topped topiary cones that briefly, arranged in this way, do look classical. And then, beyond a meadow spattered in spring with purple and white bulbs, and through a gap in a ring of trees, there is the countryside: hedges, meadows and tree clusters that seem a natural extension of this glorious Oxfordshire garden.

Gina Price's bold use of plant colour, some of which was inspired by her visits to India, might give other gardeners the confidence to experiment with unusual colour pairings of their own. A 'hot spot' of vibrant colours, such as reds, pinks, purples and orange, can work wonders in a garden that, overall, shows more restraint. If you wish to make a bold statement with colour, remember to plant in clusters and clumps to avoid a mixed tapestry look.

The Bavarian doors on the old stable building in the garden are another source of inspiration. A panel hanging on a plain wall, the door of a garden shed or summerhouse or even a length of wooden trelliswork could all be transformed into works of outdoor art with a bold geometric design and a couple of pots of weatherproof paint.

Above: Snow-covered Lower Parterre with box and yew shapes and the countryside beyond

Right: Dawn light on the borders with echinaceas, veronicastrums and *Cortaderia richardii*

THE RAWORTH GARDEN Middlesex TW1 1QS

1 mile (1.5km) from Twickenham | Open for groups of 10 or more, by appointment | Tel: 020 8892 3713 | www.raworthgarden.com

Sweetly scented old roses; an intimate Knot Garden; elegant statuary; delightful, full-to-bursting herbaceous borders; and an ingenious Bog Garden – Jenny and Richard Raworth's garden encapsulates the traditional charm and romance of an English country garden, on a ½-acre (0.2ha) London site south of the River Thames.

When the Raworths moved there 35 years ago the garden was run down and overgrown, and therefore necessitated a completely fresh start. At the time Jenny was working for London florist Malcolm Hillier, who designed the initial layout, and

the garden has been evolving ever since. The overall impression is of a quintessentially English scene with drifts of pastel pinks, blues and mauves, very little pale yellow and, Jenny insists, definitely no orange. It is beautiful.

The garden is divided into distinct areas by protective yew hedging which also assures privacy. The way the buildings – the house and the pergola – play host to prolific climbing plants means that they are absorbed into the whole garden scheme. In May the house is garlanded with pale mauve wisteria and a month later the pergola is

almost lost to view in a cloud of the dainty white 'Sander's White' rose. In front of the pergola there is a low lavender hedge planted with taller *Allium christophii* and *Iris* 'Jane Phillips'.

The one formal feature in this luxuriant scheme is a symphony in greens and cream, cool, sophisticated and intriguing. A small Knot Garden designed by Richard Raworth and their younger daughter, Kate, actually has knots! Four square parterres set in gravel paths, each with a clipped globe in the centre and composed of *Buxus sempervirens*, frame intricate, almost Celtic designs of knots

and twists shaped with *B*. 'Elegantissima Variegata' and *B*. 'Green Mountain'. In an adjacent enclosure bordering the Knot Garden, against a tall hedge of yew (*Taxus baccata*), a statue of Thisbe is flanked on each side by a terracotta pot of *Brugmansia alba*, the white, pendulous, trumpet-shaped flowers forming pretty side curtains to the central figure.

The Raworths use box and yew topiary in different sizes and in a variety of designs to give height and form and often to complement the soft, pastel-coloured planting. Without ever dominating, two tall and slender yew pillars preside over a romantic profusion of flowers in borders that edge a lawn. Two large, square stepping stones set into the grass at the edge of one border strike an interesting note of geometric hardstanding before romance takes over.

This border throbs with a delightful confusion of watercolour tints including rose-red campion (*Silene fimbriata*), red valerian (*Centranthus ruber*), the delicate, violet-blue *Geranium pratense* 'Mrs Kendall Clark', *Papaver* 'Cedric Morris', purple and white alliums and *Crambe cordifolia*. This is one of Jenny's signature plants which she especially enjoys for its misty, cloudy effect, providing height – it can grow to 6 feet (2 metres) – with such delicate transparency.

In June, when the tiny white, fragrant crambe flowers are at their prettiest, the roses proliferate in all their midsummer glory. The clear pink, bushy shrub *Rosa* 'Pink Grootendorst', the lilac-to-purple *R*. 'Reine des Violettes' and the single crimson *R*. 'Dusky Maiden', among others, make this a border to delight the senses. Short, wide topiary pyramids edge the path to the front door, the solid, green structures emphasising the subtlety of the mixed planting behind them – purple and cream irises, purple and white allium and pale pink roses.

In the garden at the front of the house, a sunken garden and a sink garden celebrate the massive array of succulents, from tiny bright-green rosettes to expansive bronze-going-on-purple ones. There is a wide variety of ways to display them, too: in sinks of all shapes, sizes and materials, terracotta dishes, bowls and tall urns. Large paving squares have gaps planted with grasses, their slender, breeze-catching foliage contrasting effectively with the large, close-to-the-ground succulents. An irregularly shaped terracotta tile makes a perfect exhibition-stand for a cluster of pinwheel succulents (*Aeonium haworthii*) with their layered rosettes of red-tinged, blue-green leaves, and a tall urn has a neat cap of closely planted golden rosettes.

And then there is the Bog Garden. This small, circular area, edged around with bricks, was once a pond but when the Raworths' first grandchild was born it was converted into a bog garden for safety considerations. However, as Jenny says, it is now so much more successful as a bog garden. Pink and purple candelabra primulas flourish beside glossy-leaved hostas in varying shades of green, and a wide, planked boardwalk, a strong feature, crosses the contained garden at a sharp angle. Facing it there is a magnificent *Cornus controversa* 'Variegata' – the wedding cake tree – favoured for its naturally tiered habit with cream flowers in spring and variegated green and white foliage which becomes fiery red in autumn.

Step inside the conservatory, originally built by Richard, on the north side of the house, and the flurry of paintbox colours is completely dazzling. Pelargoniums, fuchsia – including statuesque standard ones in pots – pink-flowered streptocarpus, violas, white roses and ferns create an aura of Edwardian grandeur. In a way, though not in its colour

Left: Thisbe is flanked by pots of pendulous angel's trumpets (*Brugmansia alba*)

Above: This border, with its watercolour tints, is 'where romance takes over'

scheme, the conservatory encapsulates the ambience of the garden as a whole – one of luxuriant profusion, planted with an artist's eye for a perfect picture.

Visit the Raworths' garden in June and you will experience the beauty and the fragrance of an abundance of old and old-fashioned roses. These are some of their favourites.

The cupped, fully-double flowers of *Rosa* 'Constance Spry', a shrub rose bred in 1960, have 'old-fashioned rose' characteristics and a strong, myrrh-like scent. *R*. 'Celeste' (syn. 'Celestial'), an old rose of unknown origin, is a classic Alba shrub rose. Its exquisite shell-pink, semi-double blooms have a sweet scent. A hybrid musk shrub rose, *R*. 'Penelope' dates from 1924. The trusses of creamy-pink flowers have a sweet fragrance. It has small coral-pink hips in autumn.

eft: The intricate design of the ironwork gate

bove: The dovecote encircled with a variety of spaliered fruit trees

One has a sense of continuity at Rousham House. The imposing, almost fortress-like acobean mansion, built on a curve on the River Cherwell, has been owned by members of the same family since Sir Robert Dormer, a staunch royalist, acquired the land in the 1630s. And the gardens, designed to complement the house and blend effortlessly into the Oxfordshire countryside, have changed little since landscape architect

William Kent completed the design over a century later. In addition, they have acquired a unique place in the history of horticultural design, being the only example of classical landscape gardens surviving almost exactly as Kent intended.

The plan for the gardens was originally laid down in the 1720s by Charles Bridgeman, a royal gardener, but it was Kent who created an Augustan landscape with features that evoke not only the glories of Renaissance Italy but also of ancient Rome. A Yorkshireman who studied art in London and moved to Italy, where for ten years

he painted frescoes, Kent envisaged this Oxfordshire garden as a landscape painting, and designed the gardens to use shape and form, light and shade to maximum effect.

He used water from springs in the hill above to create cascades, rills and ornamental pools, simple features that formed romantic cameos within the classical framework. One curvaceous rill runs through a stone channel linking the Cold Bath and the so-called Venus Vale. Other rills, sparkling and light-catching, feed into ornamental pools, and a white-water cascade tumbles into a grotto.

One large pond, surrounded by lawns and overlooked by an old stone bridge, is carpeted from side to side with waterlily leaves of stepping-stone proportions and spotlighted at times with their beautiful white, waxy flowers.

Woodland trees serve as a stage backdrop to beautifully proportioned temples, statues and follies sited at intervals along a meandering walk.

This is a walk to be taken slowly and reflectively, taking time to appreciate and assess the structures and statuary, each one given centre-stage prominence in its own glade or clearing. Some statues are fanciful or mythological, others recall Imperial Rome. There are images of Pan, of a leaping faun and of Venus. A lion savagely attacks a horse, and a gladiator, an impressive figure on an impressive plinth, is depicted in his

dying moments. A small classical temple is almost overshadowed by the arms of a large Cedar of Lebanon tree, dating from Kent's time, and unplanted urns are positioned to be appreciated as the pieces of classical sculpture they are.

William Kent's outstanding contribution to the Rousham House garden is the Praeneste, modelled on the arcaded temple at Palestrina, outside Rome, a building that was a 'must see' on the itinerary of travellers on the Grand Tour. With its seven magnificent stone arches, each framing the view beyond the sloping lawns and down to the riverside, it is not to be missed here either.

Part of the garden predates Kent's time. There is a 17th-century walled garden, productive still, and a circular dovecote still with its original revolving ladder and with espaliered fruit trees, their branches

outstretched and clinging to the walls. Around the dovecote, like pieces of a deep-green mosaic floor, is a series of hexagonal box parterres dating from Tudor times, each division now closely planted with rose bushes.

There are later additions close to the house, which in no way detract from the original design concept. In Victorian times a fernery was added, together with a conservatory to nurture frost-tender plants, and in the 20th century two long herbaceous borders were planted, adding a joyful note of informality and a palette of summer colour, and providing cut flowers for the house.

William Kent, whose nickname was 'Kentino', was fond of emphasising his classical connections by dropping Italian phrases into his conversation. When Horace Walpole (1717–97), the politician, writer and cousin of Lord Nelson, visited the estate he expressed his appreciation succinctly. Stating that he considered the Rousham House gardens the finest of all Kent's achievements, he summed them up in one word, 'Kentissimo!'

Learn from the effect that landscape designer William Kent achieved with his use of statuary at Rousham House. A piece of fine sculpture depicting a human or mythological figure or an animal, a sundial or an elegant plant container can become an eye-catching focal point in your garden and create as much impact as any flowering shrub or tree.

Consider standing your chosen piece in a niche or arch clipped from a dense hedge; at the end of the garden where two paths or hedges meet; between two trees or other features – anywhere that will draw the eye. Illogically, placing a sculpture in this way has the effect of making a garden seem longer. A delightful way to create an element of surprise is to place a sculptural piece 'round the corner' in an outside garden room where it cannot be seen from the main garden. Then stand back and wait for the oohs and aahs of visitors!

Alternatively, in another interpretation of classical garden design, position a pair of matching sculptures on either side of a door, a flight of steps, a pathway or gateway. Garden centres and specialist garden shops sell good reproductions of classical statues and other attractive garden ornaments. It is also worth looking in antique shops and in demolition yards.

Far left: The seven arches of the Praeneste, modelled on a temple at Palestrina, near Rome

Left: The gardens were designed by William Kent to use light and shade to maximum effect

Below: Graceful statues greet the visitor at every turn

SISSINGHURST CASTLE Kent TN17 2AB

2 miles (3km) north east of Cranbrook | Open selected days mid-Mar to late Oct | Tel: 01580 710700 | **www.nationaltrust.org.uk**

All established gardens have a strong sense of their own history, and nowhere is this notion of 'place' stronger than at Sissinghurst Castle. Probably one of the best known and admired gardens in the world, it is not only the breathtaking beauty of its White Garden, the Lime Walk and the Rose Garden that separately constitute its attraction. Its special character is also defined by the coherent development from 12th-century moated manor house, through Elizabethan mansion, to the romantic brick tower restored by Vita Sackville-West and her husband, Sir Harold

Nicolson, and the wonderful garden that they created.

The design of the garden is Harold Nicolson's; the planting Vita Sackville-West's, and in contrast to the linear, classical layout, the plants were encouraged to spill out over the paths and the wild flowers to set seed. The Tower Courtyard has four Irish yews underplanted with violets in spring, and rosemary 'Sissinghurst Blue' is on either side of the tower arch. Against the red Tudor brick the rose 'Allen Chandler' grows, as does a flowering quince, and there is also a trough

of blue columbines. *Magnolia grandiflora* stretches upwards, with a ceanothus and the Chilean potato tree. Running to the east of the library is the Purple Border, planted with annual and perennial shrubs in shades of blue, mauve and purple. On the opposite side of the courtyard *Hydrangea petiolaris* stands above the archway.

The Rose Garden has beds edged with box and a circular lawn, with roses trained over the central roundel. Vita Sackville-West loved old-fashioned roses, and here there are 'Fantin-Latour', 'Charles de Mills', 'Camaieux' and 'Gloire de Dijon'. Beyond this colourful garden is the Lime Walk, its long borders filled in spring with grape hyacinths, tulips, fritillaries, narcissi and anemones, backed by an avenue of pleached limes.

The Cottage Garden has a colour scheme predominantly orange, red and gold, with euphorbias, polyanthus and trollius, as well as poppies, tree peonies and the yellow-green of *Hosta fortunei* 'Aurea'.

Beyond the Moat Walk, blooming with vibrant wallflowers in summer, is the Nuttery, and further on again, the Herb Garden surrounded by yew hedges.

The Orchard, stretching down to the moat, is bright with daffodils and flowering cherries in the spring, and boasts *Rosa gallica* 'Sissinghurst Castle', an ancient variety rediscovered in 1930.

Entry to the enchanting White Garden is to the north of the formal Yew Walk, and it needs little introduction. Box hedges frame the beds which Vita Sackville-West planted in white and silver. Here, lilies, delphiniums, galtonia and speedwell, a central white rose surrounded by spiraca, pulmonaria and *Paeonia* 'Ivory Jewel' spread their magic, while a weeping pear stands sentinel beside a slender lead statue of a virgin.

With a blanket of glistening white wisteria covering the wall behind the pergola, there seems little more to be said about a garden of such beauty, except, of course: 'Go and see it for yourself!'

Left: Looking from the Rose Garden along the Yew Walk, which is lined with *Lavatera* 'Lilac Lady' and *L.* 'Barnsley'

Right: The bold blooms of *Dahlia* 'Brandaris', *Kniphofia* 'David' and *Achillea* 'Coronation Gold' light up the Cottage Garden

SPINNERS GARDEN
Hampshire SO41 5QE

2½ **miles (4km) north of Lymington** | **Open selected days Apr to Sep** | **Tel: 01590 675488** | **www.spinnersgarden.co.uk**

Standing on a wooded slope falling westward towards the Lymington River, Spinners is a garden where the spirit of the New Forest has been sympathetically preserved. It was planted by Peter Chappell over 50 years ago and is now owned by Andrew and Vicky Roberts, who continue to develop the garden to be in complete harmony with the surrounding woodland. This 2-acre (1ha) garden is full of interesting and beautiful plants, particularly those that thrive in shady conditions. Part of the garden is sheltered by a canopy of oaks, but the layout also includes an open space and a fine lawn below the house. Numerous winding paths traverse the woodland – more are frequently being added – with glades charmingly opening up at intervals.

Rhododendrons and azaleas permeate but do not dominate the woodland. In spring a fine *Rhododendron loderi* 'King George' shows its dark-pink buds, while nearby you can see *R. davidsonianum*, a triflorum with flowers that range from pink to lilac-mauve. Camellias also feature – particularly the *williamsii* hybrids – as do magnolias and lacecap and mophead hydrangeas. In spring the ground beneath the trees and shrubs is thickly carpeted with flowers, including violets, periwinkles, erythroniums, anemones, bloodroot and lungwort. Later in the summer hostas and lilies take over, supported by euphorbias, particularly *E. griffithii* 'Fireglow'. There are a number of species of dogwoods, and Japanese maples are plentiful, especially the bright-pink *Acer palmatum* 'Shishio Improved', taking over from the hydrangeas to provide a triumphant burst of colour in the autumn.

In a clearing below the steep woodland slope, fringed bleeding heart, with its blue-green leaves, is set against a berberis, while nearby there are trilliums, hellebores and pulmonaria. Cranesbill geraniums are another speciality, providing foreground planting to rare shrubs such as the purple-flowering Judas trees, magnolias and eucryphias. In a boggy area close by, ostrich ferns and periwinkles flourish, together with candelabra primulas, lysichiton, moisture-loving iris and other suitable inhabitants of the bog garden. The stone path that runs behind the house leads to an area with tree peonies, euphorbias, day lilies and lady's smock. Above the plant sales area there is a small path which runs among many varieties of erythroniums and passes a small example of *Rhododendron roxieanum oreonastes*, which has glossy, narrow leaves and creamy flowers. To the south of the nursery is an open area where an outstanding magnolia can be seen, *Magnolia x loebneri* 'Leonard Messel', with lilac-pink flowers.

Although Spinners is a relatively small garden, it has much to inspire and delight the plant-lover throughout the seasons and, as more and more areas are planted, will be of renewed interest year by year.

Left: Foliage shape and colour are skilfully contrasted

Above: Spinners captures the spirit of the New Forest

WALES & THE MARCHES | 3

If there is one common factor that links gardens in this chapter, it must surely be their diversity. There are examples of exuberant, exciting, colourful Arts and Crafts planting and, by contrast, a garden with structured, verdant planting that could scarcely be more formal. Add to that a botanic garden, a watery wonderland created beneath the ground, a showcase of acid-loving plants – rhododendrons and camellias especially – and a masterclass in vertical planting and the visitor to this region is spoilt for choice.

BODNANT GARDEN Conwy LL28 5RE

6 miles (9.5km) south of Conwy | Open daily Mar to Dec | Tel: 01492 650460 | **www.bodnant-garden.co.uk**

Set high above the River Conwy with spectacular views over the magnificent Snowdonia range, Bodnant is considered by many people to be the finest garden in Britain. It is famous for its collections of rhododendrons, camellias and magnolias which in the spring and early summer turn it into a dazzling kaleidoscope of colour. There are other equally breathtaking features to enjoy, too: the stunning sight of a long tunnel positively cascading with laburnum racemes in early summer, and the Lily Terrace pond, its surface broken up by many rare waterlilies.

Bodnant was first established when Henry Pochin planted the conifers in 1875, but it was his daughter, the 1st Lady Aberconway, who extended the garden to include herbaceous borders and shrubs as well as trees. In 1949 the 2nd Lord Aberconway gave the 80 acres (32.5ha) of Bodnant Garden to the National Trust.

On crossing the front lawn, the eye is immediately captured by the enormous range of colour in the adjoining beds provided by many different shrubs, among them ceanothus, choisyas, hydrangeas and many clematis, including 'Marcel Moser' and 'Gipsy Queen'. The Rose Terrace offers what is probably the finest view in Bodnant Garden, with the Snowdonia range providing the backdrop to rose beds edged with saxifrages, helianthemums, dwarf campanulas and the soft-textured *Stachys lanata*. Around the walls are rhododendrons, *Mahonia* 'Charity', a row of *Camellia x williamsii* and a splendid pieris with deep-red new leaves in April and August.

A flight of steps leading down to the Croquet Terrace brings you to a wisteria-clothed fountain and several beautiful shrubs including *Eucryphia x nymansensis* 'Nymansay', which has clusters of large

white flowers in late summer, and numerous viburnums; indeed – of particular interest to the plant enthusiast – the Bodnant Garden holds the national collection of eucryphias. Continuing downwards, you reach the third terrace with its lily pond and great cedar trees where the buttressed walls provide shelter for hydrangeas, ceanothus and *Camellia reticulata*.

Four big beds of roses occupy the Lower Rose Terrace and, on each side, a pergola covered with clematis leads down to the Canal Terrace, its lawns bordered by beds of purple, blue and grey herbaceous plants, and by hedges and trees. At one end stands the Pin Mill, an attractive gazebo dating from 1730, and at the other a raised lawn serves as a stage.

Below the canal is the final terrace which boasts a multitude of magnolias, including *Magnolia kobus*, *M. sinensis*, and *M. wilsonii*. The view back towards the house is one of Italian formality, a sharp contrast with the woodland garden dotted with rhododendrons, camellias, azaleas and hydrangeas which clothe the valley right down to the river.

The view to the distant mountains is always exhilarating, but arguably never more so than in autumn when the peaks are seen beyond a foreground of trees in varying shades of reds, greens, purples and golds. Time for a photograph!

There are many gardens with secret 'rooms' concealing architectural and horticultural delights; but none, surely, with the magic and mystery that await the visitor to Dewstow. The white-painted 19th-century house, standing on a rise, is surrounded by tidy lawns, rock gardens, a string of pools linked by streams and a border colour-bright with perennials and bulbs – delphiniums and sisyrinchium, alliums and lilies; 6 acres (2.5ha) in all. The views across the Severn estuary are magnificent.

This attractive but almost conventional garden is but an interesting curtain-raiser for what lies beneath the ground, a labyrinth of passages and pools, grottoes and caverns, waterfalls and rills, excavated and created because of one man's passion for ferns and tropical plants.

Henry Roger Keane Oakley, a director of Great Western Railway, bought the Dewstow estate in 1893 and, with incredible vision and determination, embarked on creating a natural-looking habitat for his extensive plant collection. It is thought that this man-made environment, on this scale, has no equal anywhere in the world.

Even today, there is a frisson of anticipation as one starts to explore this subterranean oasis. Steps flanked by a sturdy balustrade lead down to a mysterious environment where there are dimly lit grottoes, water trickling down rocky walls and a large pond with a noisy waterfall. Ferns thrive in these man-made conditions and grow out between rocks, here, there,

Left: The fountain in the Duck Pond

Below: Border above the croquet lawn with a lush planting of *Cosmos* 'Gazebo Mixed', *Crocosmia* 'Lucifer', *Stachys byzantina*, rudbeckia, heuchera and persicaria

Right: The sunken area above the Square Garden

and everywhere. Then, around a corner, there is a large, lush fernery that was once topped by a large glass dome. Massive columns support the roof of a large rectangular grotto and a stream snakes through the centre. Rock-slab stepping stones bridge narrow channels of fast-flowing water and a group of 'stalactites' almost touches the surface of a green-dark pool. Waterlilies cover the surface of other pools. Sunlight streaks through gaps in the walls. Rocks are moss-covered or tightly

bound around with clinging evergreen plants; some almost block one's progress. All is not quite what it seems. Many of the rocks, pillars and apparent stalactites were constructed of a sand and cement mix known as Pulhamite spread over base shapes. One would never know.

There is a sudden burst of colour – a free-standing table-sized rock has a cushion of brilliant pink alpines – and a tropical garden has the lush ambience one associates with a rain forest. The moisture-loving plants in a bog garden include the giant *Gunnera manicata*, candelabra primulas, rodgersia, iris and a variety of grasses.

Squire Oakley, as he was known, died in the 1940s, after which the gardens and grottoes were allowed to fall into disrepair. Worse still, soil from excavations for the nearby M4 motorway were dumped on the site and the underground caverns and passages became little more than local folk memory. That was until the Harris family partnership bought the estate in 1999 and, while clearing part of the garden, John Harris discovered a flight of steps at the foot of a bank and a blocked passage leading to the grottoes.

One discovery led to another and over the following decade the Harrises and their friends spent the winters excavating and restoring the caves as authentically as possible, and employed a head gardener to recreate the gardens and ferneries with the plant species that Squire Oakley would have used.

Now the gardens and grottoes are almost back to the glory days of their creation in the late-Victorian era.

Left: View out of the garden to the Second Severn Crossing beyond

Right: A fairy nymph hides behind a waterfall in the Tufa Grotto

DYFFRYN GARDENS
Vale of Glamorgan CF5 6SU

7 miles (11.25km) south west of Cardiff | Usually open daily all year | Tel: 029 2059 3328 | **www.dyffryngardens.com**

There has been a mansion at Dyffryn, just to the west of Cardiff, since the end of the 16th century; both the present house and the fascinating botanic gardens that surround it date from Edwardian times.

John Cory built the house, and his third son, Reginald, a well-known figure in horticultural circles, commissioned Thomas Mawson, the leading landscape architect of his generation, to design the 55-acre (22ha) gardens between 1906 and 1914.

The Pompeian Garden with its impressive collection of statuary is based on gardens seen by the two men on their Grand Tour in the early 20th century.

Reginald Cory had a particular interest in the cultivation of dahlias and during his time at Dyffryn trialled 7,000 dahlia plants spanning 1,000 cultivars. In 1927 he joined Major Lawrence Johnston, who created the garden at Hidcote Manor, on a plant-hunting expedition to South Africa and was known for

the generous distribution of his discoveries to other gardeners and to botanical gardens. Cory also specialised in plants from China and Japan, many of which were introduced to Europe by plant collector E H Wilson for the first time at Dyffryn. Today, much of the fascination of the gardens reflects those early interests, in the many impressive Oriental trees and shrubs, including the two large paperbark maples *Acer griseum*, and the Chusan palms in the arboretum.

In front of the house is a stunning waterlily canal, surrounded by a great lawn. To the west is a series of 'garden rooms' enclosed by yew hedges, each one with a different theme. There is a Roman Garden, for instance, and a circular Fuchsia Garden which was originally the Rose Garden, plus – a favourite of the Edwardians – an open-air theatre. Beyond, winding walks lead through the informal West Garden, past splendid vistas between colourful beds of herbaceous shrubs and flowers, with magnolias providing a magnificent display in spring and early summer. The Vine Walk is at its best in autumn when the striking foliage colours capture the eye.

In its heyday the Walled Garden would have played a vital part in the daily life of the household, supplying exotic fruit, vegetables and flowers for the house, but for years it had fallen into disuse and disrepair and had not been accessible to the general public. However, an ambitious restoration scheme has brought this 2-acre (0.8ha) site back to life. About one quarter of the area is taken up by two new glasshouses producing, as in earlier times, heritage fruit and vegetables in one and exotic plants including cacti and rare orchids in the other. Archaeological work on the site uncovered two original dipping ponds that were used for watering and washing plants; these will now be reinstated into the overall scheme of the kitchen garden.

This is a garden of cohesive contrasts which is being sympathetically and authentically restored. The 110-yard (100-metre) herbaceous borders, among the longest known in the country; the immaculate lawns punctuated by geometric paths and lines of tall topiary cones; the romantic walk beneath rose-covered arches: this garden is a feast for every one of the senses.

Left: This statue of Chinese philosopher Lao-tse on a water buffalo was presented to the gardens in the 1950s

Above: Magnificent twin borders in this Grade I-listed Edwardian garden

Below: East meets west: a formal pool with dwarf acers and overhanging wisteria

HIGH GLANAU MANOR Mons NP25 4AD

4 miles (6.5km) south west of Monmouth | Open for National Garden Scheme (NGS) and by appointment | Tel: 01600 860005

The Arts and Crafts manor house at Lydart has that most desirable of all attributes: location, location, location. Situated high up on a hillside, the property is revealed at the end of a road enclosed on both sides by tall trees. It is as if this tunnel-like approach were designed to heighten the wow factor. It does; just as certainly as the situation of the house was selected to make the most of the truly breathtaking views over the Vale of Usk to Sugar Loaf and the Brecon Beacons.

The house and garden were designed in the 1920s as one entity, each perfectly complementing the other, by Henry Avray Tipping, an authority on the history and architecture of English houses and their gardens. Tipping worked alongside Gertrude Jekyll and was a friend of Harold Peto and so it is likely that he was influenced by the work of these two great garden designers.

This was Tipping's last Monmouthshire home; he died in 1933. Over time the garden had fallen into disrepair and many of its characteristic features had become indistinguishable. It was not until 2002 when the Manor was bought by Helena and Hilary Gerrish that the garden, Tipping's garden, began to come to life again. Helena Gerrish has made it her determined ambition to restore not only its beauty but its integrity, and she has achieved so much already that it is possible now to walk across the terraces, down the steps, along the paths and view the house, the plantings and the surrounding landscape much as Tipping himself would have done.

It is a feature of Arts and Crafts houses that the garden begins at the house; it is wrapped around it. High Glanau Manor is no exception. Wisteria clads the walls, a white door is almost enwrapped by purple clematis and pink roses, and foxgloves and other cottage-garden plants edge a terrace. This softening-of-the-outlines effect is evident throughout the garden: a part-cladding of moss is welcome on stone walls; topiary balls of clipped box surmount stone pillars; a helter-skelter topiary structure presides over a stout plinth; the stone steps leading down to an octagonal pool are fringed with lavender; and the pool itself is ringed around with roses – architecture and planting in perfect harmony.

The highlight of the garden, and surely Helena Gerrish's greatest achievement to date, is the replanting in a single season of the 100-foot (30-metre) double herbaceous borders that, separated by a wide grass path, form painterly lines between the house and the pergola. Working from old photographs of Tipping's garden, Helena has faithfully replicated his original planting scheme using the subtle colour blends that typify the taste of the Edwardian era. Towering blue delphiniums and paler blue iris, lime-yellow euphorbia and lady's mantle with an underplanting of white – the effect is beautiful. Helena used old photographs, too, to renovate the pergola. With a little restoration the stone pillars, now criss-crossed with clematis and roses, have withstood the test of time and sturdy wooden beams support the climbing plants.

A gate in a wall leads to the Kitchen Garden, productive again with young fruit trees and organic vegetables, and to the greenhouse, another restoration project achieved with the aid of photographic reference. As elegant now as it ever was, and embraced by an old vine, the greenhouse makes it possible to bring forward the seasonal harvests of tomatoes, herbs and squashes and provide early tulips for the house.

This is a hillside garden of many levels. Another gate leads down to a lower terrace encroached by planting in typically Arts and Crafts colours – orange, yellows and blues, achieved with kniphofia, lilies and delphiniums, and a small pond has an island bed planted with the contrasting colours and forms of hostas and azaleas. Then, further downhill, a lane bisects this 12-acre (5ha) garden and, over the way, there are walks on the wild side, through woodland and down to the river, streams and sparkling waterfalls.

Tipping's original planting of rhododendrons is enhanced in spring by a carpet of bluebells – a glorious sight.

Left: Red Valerian adds colour to the upper terrace, where a table is set up for an al fresco meal

Below: View from the terrace to the landscape beyond

HODNET HALL Shropshire TF9 3NN

6 miles (9.5km) south west of Market Drayton | Open some Sundays Jun–Jul; groups by appointment | Tel: 01630 685786 | **www.hodnethallgardens.org**

Situated in the lovely rolling countryside of mid-Shropshire, Hodnet Hall is surrounded by 60 acres (24ha) of magnificent gardens. The red-brick house was built in 1870 in the later Elizabethan style; below it is a central pool which is the beginning of a chain of lakes running down to the west. These lakes not only create the main axis of the garden, but establish the theme of the garden as a whole.

In 1922, when the pool was little more than a marshy hollow surrounded by elders, laurel and rushes, the present owner's father, Brigadier A G W Heber-Percy, turned what had been his full-time hobby into a gardening career in order to make Hodnet Hall pay its way. In this lime-free environment he created a series of lakes which are thought to be one of the largest water gardens in the country, and filled the grounds with the bright colours of acid-loving plants including camellias and rhododendrons.

Moving west from the forecourt of the house, you soon come to the entrance to the Woodland Garden with its rhododendrons, specimen trees and spring bulbs that make such an attractive show. Round the side of the private garden is the

Broad Walk, which runs along the south front of the house, offering a fine view over the lake and the surrounding fields to a dovecote built in 1656. Before reaching the Rose Garden you pass the terrace borders, and the slope beyond is planted with Japanese maples, *Acer* 'Dissectum Atropurpureum' and *A. palmatum* 'Palmatifidum', with the rhododendrons 'Tortoiseshell Champagne', 'Mrs A T de la Mare', 'The Master' and 'Princess Anne', as well as *Berberis stenophylla* and *Kalmia latifolia*.

The outer ring of the Rose Garden is planted with a collection of old-fashioned roses including 'Comte de Chambord', 'Rose de Resht', 'Felicia' and 'Penelope'. Inside, mixed peonies provide stunning colour around a central bed with a statue, planted with hydrangeas. Crossing a bridge through the Lower Rose Garden and the Camellia Garden, shining with varieties such as 'Donation' and 'Cornish Snow', you soon find yourself almost absorbed by the giant-leaved gunneras of a water garden underplanted with candelabra primulas, irises and great drifts of astilbes.

There is much to see at Hodnet Hall, a garden that has been carefully planted to provide colour throughout the year. The daffodils, blossom and bulbs make a brave show in the spring, soon to be followed by rhododendrons, azaleas, lilacs and laburnum. July brings the magnificent roses which contrast with the more vibrant colour of fuchsias, while August is the perfect time for the water plants. The season concludes with the colourful berries and bright foliage of acers, berberis and sorbus.

Left: The central pool below the house is the first of a series of lakes which, together, form what is thought to be one of the largest water gardens in the country

Above: When spring is in the air the gardens are colour-bright with rhododendrons and azaleas

RIDLER'S GARDEN Swansea SA2 0FW

Completely enclosed by meticulously manicured hedges, Ridler's Garden is an oasis of supreme tranquillity – a delightful discovery, in view of its close proximity to an urban environment. And it is a precision garden of almost perfect symmetry. The owner ensures this by buying plants in twos, fours and sixes. There is not a leaf out of place, and with so many clipped hedges and innovative topiary shapes there are a great many leaves. Paths lead directly to sculptures and other decorative or architectural features and it is as if the eye dare not wander.

Tony Ridler, a graphic designer, has created the garden over some 18 years. He has the patience to wait while hedges develop as he intends them to, and for seven years until standard hollies are tall and thick enough to shape like lollipops. But he is restless with the effect created in some areas and never reluctant to make changes. And so any description of his garden is likely to go rapidly out of date.

The long narrow plot which widens at the end is completely enclosed on all sides. It has a formal framework of paths, many of them veritable works of paving art because

of the ingenious way natural and recycled materials have been used together to create intricate patterns and textural contrasts. Dressed stone taken from a deconsecrated chapel, old paving stones, cobbles, railway sleepers, granite and chunks of wood salvaged from the Swansea dockyard set the stage for the real stars of this garden – the topiary.

Clipped yew, box and holly hedges divide the garden into separate rooms and define the gradual changes in the level. Walking from one enclosed area to the next one wonders how much more can be achieved with topiary; how many more effects and representations can be wrought from the evergreen plants.

One area enclosed by yew walls and divided by a central path has rows of box clipped into helter-skelter shapes which represent shells, a reference to the cockle-fishing industry of Penclawdd on the Glamorganshire coast. In further tribute, the evergreen shapes are planted in beds covered with cockle shells.

A narrow path leads through an avenue of mop-headed Portugal laurels (*Prunus lusitanica*) underplanted with edge-to-edge box balls. These hummocky shapes form scalloped lines along their tops and catch the light in intriguing ways, creating uniform patterns of light and shade. Beyond the 'ball park' is another, more open enclosure with four lawn segments each planted with an elegant weeping ash and, beyond them, a dark-blue door with faux steps made of clipped box. Standard hollies stand guard on either side.

At the head of a gravel path there is a large red sandstone ammonite sculpture mounted on a tall, narrow block of wood retrieved from Swansea pier, and another path is interrupted by a monolith on a stepped box plinth flanked by red-flowering standard camellias.

There is scant need for the intrusion of flowers in any quantity to disturb the rhythm of this evergreen, geometric garden.

One artistic exception is a large horizontal stencilled panel depicting blue, mauve, pink and white hellebores on a matt black wall. A thick ribbon of hellebores is planted beneath it.

Other flowers are occasionally permitted. Tony Ridler plants 500 parrot tulips to flower in spring and species lilies that will radiate colour in summer. However, they are hidden away behind a hedge.

Left: View along the path to the far-off blue bench with yew hedges, clipped box, rocks and *Iris sibirica* in between

Below: The vegetable garden is planted with alliums, box cones, figs and yew hedges

STONE HOUSE COTTAGE

Worcs DY10 4BG

2 miles (3km) south east of Kidderminster | **Open selected days mid-Mar to mid-Sep** | **Tel: 01562 69902** | **www.shcn.co.uk**

Seeing is not always – at first sight, anyway – believing. It seems that the towers and domes, pillars and shelters that make up the architectural structure of Stone House Cottage Garden have been in place for centuries. In fact, they have all been skilfully constructed by James Arbuthnott, an amateur builder, since he and his wife Louisa, a knowledgeable plantswoman, bought the property in 1974. At that time it was a run-down kitchen garden with little more

than red-brick Victorian perimeter walls and a gardener's cottage. Louisa saw the walls as potential support and protection for a profusion of climbing plants – there are now over 120 different varieties – and cover for shade-loving ones. And the Arbuthnotts both saw the opportunity to develop a high-end plant nursery, which is now well established close to the car park.

There were two immediate priorities: to clear the site and draw up a ground

plan, putting their long-term vision on paper. That vision has now been gloriously realised and the results are there for all to see. The garden has been sub-divided into small 'rooms', using mainly yew (*Taxus baccata*), purple-leaved plum (*Prunus cerasifera* 'Pissardii') and box (*Buxus sempervirens*). The construction of these living walls makes for an intriguing layout that promises a new vista at every turn. Linked by grass paths – corridors – that

criss-cross the garden, the rooms display a variety of planting schemes. One, close to the entrance folly, is planted as a shady woodland garden where, growing among long grass, shrubs have a naturalised look. Here they include the white-flowering *Viburnum plicatum* 'Mariesii', the Chinese persimmon *Diospyros kaki* – laden with yellowy-orange fruits in late summer – and *Dipelta floribunda* with its peeling, pale-brown bark and fragrant, pale-pink flowers.

Go through a neat archway in the yew hedging and you come to herbaceous borders displaying rare and specimen plants in striking colour mixtures. One group, for example, boasts a yellow, crimson and blue palette carried out with the showy yellow flowers of *Dicentra macrantha*, the brilliant crimson, almost spherical blooms of

Knautia macedonica and towering spires of *Delphinium* 'Alice Artindale', whose double, rosy-mauve and sky-blue flowers make this a plant to covet.

Height is important in this garden; dominant, even. With the in-situ brick walls and James's architectural features in place, Louisa could indulge her passion for unusual climbers and wall shrubs and experiment with some whose hardiness was in doubt. Flowering times are carefully taken into account. For example, on one wall *Clianthus puniceus*, the New Zealand parrot's bill which produces waxy, scarlet flowers in spring, is planted close to *Dregea sinensis*, whose red and cream flowers follow on in summer. Geographical borders are routinely crossed as the Japanese loquat, *Eriobotrya japonica*, flourishes alongside the South American *Azara microphylla* 'Variegata' – favoured for

its characteristic vanilla-like fragrance – and *Mitraria coccinea* 'Lake Puyehue' which, originating from the cold forests of southern Chile, has red and yellow tubular fruits that span three seasons.

Identification is facilitated in these inspirational gardens as the hundreds of climbers, small trees, shrubs and herbaceous plants are clearly labelled; and, with Louisa Arbuthnott on hand to give advice on aspect and soil preferences, visitors have a fine opportunity to plot their own visionary garden.

Left: Criss-crossing paths serve as corridors between the rooms, revealing a new vista every time

Above: These walls are made for climbing – for over 120 different varieties of climbing plants, that is

VEDDW GARDEN

Monmouthshire NP16 6PH

5 miles (8km) north west of Chepstow | Open Sunday afternoons Jun to Aug | Tel: 01291 650836 | **www.veddw.com**

This is a garden that is not only in sympathy with the surrounding Welsh-border countryside; in parts it has been cleverly designed by its owners, Charles Hawes and Anne Wareham, to echo it. A range of waist-high box hedges, looking from a distance somewhat like an angular maze, follows the lines of hedgerows marked on an 1841 tithe map of the settlement.

As a tribute to both the history of the landscape and the present views of farmland beyond the garden, these enclosures, themselves surrounded by taller yew hedges and forming a kind of parterre, are treated as fields in miniature and planted appropriately with ornamental grasses – an ideal filling for any parterre, as many of them look their best in blocks.

By contrast, the New Garden, completed in 2010, has straight lines of grasses, *Allium* 'Purple Sensation', *Geranium macrorrhizum* and *Campanula lactiflora*, which are seen in tiers from a comfortable large black seat.

The Cornfield Garden has small formal beds contained by box and fencing containing *Calamagrostis x acutiflora* 'Karl Foerster', again as an echo of the surrounding agricultural landscape.

The Hedge Garden echoes the characteristics of the countryside in a further way. Its clipped yew hedges have undulating tops following the lines of the long, low curves of the Welsh border hills. A large rectangular reflecting pool presents a mirror image of the Hedge Garden with the coppice and forest trees behind it, and the back of a long, low pink seat has the signature Veddw garden sinuous curves.

On a steep slope to the east of the enclosures a grass parterre is created with box hedges in-filled with a mixture of ornamental grasses including blue-green festuca, deschampsia (tufted hair-grass) and stipa, whose sandy-brown spikelets last well into winter. Yew domes rising from the gentle waves of grasses provide additonal year-round structural interest.

In winter, when this evergreen ground plan is veiled in snow or rimed with heavy frost, the layout of the garden is even more distinct and dramatic, taking on the intensity of a black-and-white photograph.

Early summer through to late autumn is when the crescent border at the foot of the Hedge Garden is at its most vibrant and photogenic. Tall yew hedges form a framework against which Anne plants perennials in soft colours with ornamental grasses such as miscanthus mingling with campanula, *Epilobium angustifolium* 'Stahl Rose' and roses.

The vegetable garden brings about an attractive fusion of opposites with standard hollies and box balls in formal beds, and many-coloured clematis colonising vertical supports. Cardoons and purple heuchera are Charles' statement plants of choice, backed by purple and silver shrubs – an inspirational blend of formality and individuality.

There are many other inspirational borders and features within the Veddw plan that are worth taking note of. A good example is the grey border backed by *Rosa* 'Felicia' and buddleia, where in late summer Japanese anemones add a touch of pink to silver-grey foliage plants. There is also the charmingly named 'Froth' Garden, planted with mainly pink roses, geraniums, hydrangea and heuchera, its romantically pretty colouring punctuated by hostas.

The meadow is spattered with bulbs in spring and then, reminiscent of the countryside long ago, with wild flowers in summer, and the 'step' borders feature giant hostas mingling with crocosmia and day lilies.

Left: Box balls and wayward cardoons: the attraction of opposites

Above: The garden is at its most dramatic when clothed in winter hoar frost

Below: Breathtaking autumn colours create a stunning display

WOLLERTON OLD HALL

Shropshire TF9 3NA

½ mile (0.8km) north east of Hodnet | Open selected days Easter to Sep | Tel: 01630 685760 | www.wollertonoldhallgarden.com

Left: Pyramids of clipped yew dwarf a stone basin

Above: *Erysimum* 'Apricot Delight', *Salvia nemorosa* 'Caradonna' and *Achillea* 'Coronation Gold' in the 'hot' border

On a five-centuries-old site the new garden surrounding the 16th-century hall house achieves a skilful blend of formal and informal, of restrained but most of all flamboyant planting. At times the colour in this 4-acre (1.6ha) garden is breathtaking. Here is a relatively newly planted garden on a site where there has probably been one since 1530. It is designed in the classical English Arts and Crafts style and uses colour in a way that seems oddly familiar. Could it

be that it resembles the decoration on some of Clarice Cliff's more exuberant pieces?

The garden surrounds the black-and-white half-timbered house where Lesley Jenkins lived as a child. When she and her husband John moved to the property in 1983 they found an almost completely empty field of about 3 acres. Over the next 20 years, Lesley Jenkins set about designing the garden with an emphasis on colour and form, integrating indigenous and rare plant species and embracing both hot and cool themes.

The geometric lines of the house suggest a sympathetic symmetry in the garden design, thus boundaries are defined by brick walls and long straight hedges, mainly of beech and yew. On the site of the

original Elizabethan knot garden, the area now described as the 'Old Garden' has a crenellated York stone path flanked by two lines of mophead standards of Portugal laurel (*Prunus lusitanica*) enlivened in spring by ground-covering harebells and camomile.

Giving perspective to the central vista, the Lime Allee is planted with pleached limes, *Tilia platyphyllos* 'Rubra', and delightfully underplanted with *Viola labradorica* and *Muscari latifolium,* which in summer is followed by the understated *Heliotropium* 'Lord Roberts'.

The entrance to the Yew Walk is colourfully announced for several weeks of the year by two oak balustrades curtained in clematis, including 'Black Madonna',

'Romantika', Negritjanka' and *Clematis fusca* var. *violacea*. The pyramidal yews lining the avenue stand in soldierly rows, evergreen sculptures forming bays planted with drifts of perennials in white and yellow with the odd 'trumpets' coming from splashes of purple, blue and orange.

Colour is used to dramatic effect in the main perennial border which is protected by an old brick wall and accessed through a gate cascading with honeysuckle. Here the planting is in well-defined diagonal drifts, colour merging into colour, in the manner characteristic of the famed garden designer Gertrude Jekyll. Many species, delphiniums, veronicastrum, monardas amongst them, are set in clusters of up to 11 plants: strong statements, not spatterings of colour. The room known as the Daisy Borders, with a sundial set in the centre of a wide grass path and with twin borders packed with aquilegia, delphiniums, hollyhocks and asters, has a look of autonomy. It could be any small and beautiful English garden anywhere. However, it is intended that this area will soon be integrated with an adjacent garden to create a large Rose and Perennial Garden.

Colour runs riot in many areas; never more so than in the Lanhydrock Garden which explodes into view through a gap in a tall beech screen. Here it is bold and certainly beautiful. Colour-wise, August is the hottest month, beginning with the opening firework-like display of Oriental poppies before fiery dahlias in flame, coral, red and orange take up the theme. Rudbeckias, red-going-on-golden helenium and lastly a significant collection of salvias maintain the wow factor which, here, is maximised.

There are two water features at Wollerton Old Hall, each with totally different characteristics. One, approached through an ivy-festooned door, has a central limestone well head flanked by more pyramid-shaped yews, as if they are standing formal guard over this ancient water source. Picking up the colour theme from the sparkling effect of sun on clear water, peripheral planting around the well marries white and pale lemon-yellow with apricot in the form of *Rosa* 'Lady Emma Hamilton'. By contrast, the sound of more running water leads one to a tranquil area where, in a rectangular sunken garden, there is a rill running over York stone. A newer, upper rill is directed through a canal edged with fat hummocks of clipped box. Giving the opportunity for rest and reflection there is, nearby, an oak gazebo hooded in *Rosa* 'Champney's Pink Cluster', supporting *Clematis crispa*.

A magnificent oak loggia with the look of ages offers similar pause for thought, facing as it does an old stone font rising up, in spring, from surrounding waves of delicate *Fritillaria meleagris*. Once the fritillaries are dormant they are replaced in early summer by moon daisies (*Leucanthemum vulgare*).

After so many intimate, secluded and diverse 'rooms', the garden eventually comes down to earth and mingles with the world outside, the hills and vales of the Shropshire countryside close to Market Drayton, where there was a Saxon settlement. Norwegian maples and mature specimen shrubs including the winter- and early spring-flowering *Stachyurus chinensis*, as well as later delights such as *Hoheria* 'Glory of Amlwch' and *Heptacodium miconioides*, known as seven-son flower, finally bring down the curtain on a garden in which so many exciting elements compete for attention.

Right: Planting in drifts to achieve strong statements of colour creates maximum impact throughout this Arts and Crafts garden

CENTRAL ENGLAND & EAST ANGLIA | 4

Within Central England and East Anglia lie some of Britain's most beautiful and unspoilt counties, where fertile fens border ancient market towns and chocolate-box villages. This region has a wealth of interest for garden visitors all the year round. From a garden that momentarily attracts the passing attention of north–south railway passengers to others that, true to their medieval roots and even favoured by royalty, are a significant part of Britain's heritage and offer a walk back through time; gardens that, through their sub-tropical planting, spectacularly defy the vagaries of an inhospitable climate and ones where a warm welcome is assured even in deepest winter.

COTTESBROOKE HALL Northamptonshire NN6 8PF

8 miles (13km) north of Northampton | **Open selected days May to Sep** | **Tel: 01604 505808** | **www.cottesbrookehall.co.uk**

To the north of Northampton, in that secluded countryside which saw the Civil War battle of Naseby, is the early 18th-century Cottesbrooke Hall. The building commenced in 1702 for Sir John Langham, 4th Baronet, and concluded in 1713. The original architect was Francis Smith of Warwick and the house has remained essentially the same ever since, with minor alterations by Robert Mitchell at the end of the 18th century. The approach over the classical Mitchell Bridge offers a spectacular view of the house.

The splendid parkland remains almost unchanged since it was laid out in the English style during the 18th century, but the gardens have developed over the past 100 years and have flourished under the tenure of the current owners, the Macdonald-Buchanan family. The formal gardens are still held together by the strong influence from the Arts and Crafts Movement and are continually being updated and developed by a number of influential designers. The result is a series of charming enclosed courtyards and gardens around the house, immaculately maintained by the present owners, Mr and Mrs Alastair Macdonald-Buchanan, and their head gardener, Mr Phylip Statner.

On entering the garden opposite the west wing, there is a magnificent view of the lake and of Brixworth Church, which dates originally from Anglo-Saxon times. A large tulip tree, an *Acer griseum* and several magnolias can be seen. The forecourt created by the English landscape architect Sir Geoffrey Jellicoe (1900–96) highlights his love of the Baroque style; the influence of Italian gardens is evident through the restrained use of stone and lead decorations. Beyond the wrought-iron gates is the Statue Walk, with the Belgian sculptor Peter Scheemakers's four statues from the Temple of Ancient Virtue at Stowe, backed by clipped yews. Opposite the statues and either side of the Eagle Gates is a herbaceous border designed by the Chelsea award-winning garden designer Arne Maynard featuring large wisterias and planted in a wonderful, soft romantic style. This gate leads into the Pool Garden which houses an elegant shelter designed by Dame Sylvia Crowe, the British landscape architect (1901–97).

The Pine Court is dominated by an old Scots pine with a climbing hydrangea, and the Dutch Garden, with its two sundials, is planted with spectacular spring and summer bedding. Around every corner is a wonderful surprise. The 71-yard-long (65-metre) double herbaceous terrace borders redesigned by James Alexander Sinclair have an unconventional and informal planting style and are overlooked by an ancient cedar of Lebanon tree.

Extending to 13 acres (5.25ha), the gardens capture a variety of moods and display a variety of planting styles. In addition to those described there is the Spinney Garden and two wild gardens, planted with azaleas, rhododendrons, primroses and daffodils whilst hostas, hellebores, ligularias and astilbes grow in profusion by the bridge. In contrast to the orderliness of the formal gardens, one long border in the Wild Garden is thickly planted with giant gunnera forming a dense wall outlining the woodland beyond.

Left: Fabulous colour in the double borders lining the path up to the house

Below: This view from the roof shows the wonderful parkland surrounding Cottesbrooke Hall

CROSSING HOUSE Cambridgeshire SG8 6PS

8 miles (13km) south of Cambridge | Usually open daily all year | Tel: 01763 261071

Although the garden at Crossing House is small it is packed with interest, variety and colour and there is plenty to inspire and encourage owners of other gardens where space is limited. Cultivated for over half a century by Mr and Mrs Douglas Fuller and now co-owned by John Marlar, who helps them to maintain it, the garden must be one of the best known in the country, standing as it does beside a level crossing at Shepreth on the King's Cross–Cambridge railway line. It is tempting to reflect just how much over the years this tiny cultivated area must have lifted the spirits of travellers on the busy commuter line and how many, on other occasions, have interrupted their journey to have a closer look at the garden.

Mrs Fuller's aim was to ensure that visitors – and even passers-by – would have something of value and interest to see throughout the year. This aim has been richly fulfilled: there are many species to be seen all year round and the greenhouses are packed with orchids and tender bulbs. Bulb experts have identified 35 varieties of snowdrop and snowflake at Crossing House, giant forms and those with green and yellow tips, growing amongst aconites, whilst early spring produces drifts of naturalised bulbs including *Crocus tommasinianus*

'Whitewell Purple', scilla and chionodoxa, which provide a background for dwarf tulips and daffodils. As the season progresses these are succeeded by alliums, trilliums, lilies and hardy terrestrial orchids, some with spectacular spikes of bright purple and mauve flowers.

Clematis and peonies provide a wealth of summer colour, and there is an abundance of roses, many of which are delightfully fragrant. Raised limestone beds hold alpines. During the autumn, Japanese anemones, colchicums, phlox and Michaelmas daisies are as eye-catching as any summer display, while varieties of *Camellia sasanqua* with their white, red and pink flowers flourish on a raised acid bed. Even in winter there is much to see, even from a distance: the exquisite colours and forms of rare hellebores, the bright-as-beacons early crocus and dainty dwarf irises are all in flower during a mild period, as are the more showy witch hazels, mahonias, viburnums and winter jasmine. A pond and two fountains are well established at Crossing House, and in the greenhouses Douglas Fuller grows streptocarpus, rare orchids and southern hemisphere bulbs, many of which he has raised from seed.

It is truly remarkable what the Fullers have achieved in a small space in this rail-side country garden, from the precision of the dwarf box edging to the profusion of flower-filled beds; from impressive yew arches to fine-tuned topiary. The beauty of this garden must surely give encouragement and pleasure to visitors all year round and, fleetingly but just as importantly, to passing travellers too.

Left: A train passing perilously near the house and its surprisingly tranquil garden

Right: A topiary horse is a talking point

145

DOCWRA'S MANOR Hertfordshire SG8 6PS

8 miles (13km) south west of Cambridge | Open selected days all year | Tel: 01763 260677 | www.docwrasmanorgarden.co.uk

The planting in Docwra's Manor garden is inspired. One can search for a formula and not find one. The borders are a tapestry of mixed colours, but not too mixed. Flower colours are principally blue, mauve, white and pink with significant additions of grey-leaved plants, cotton thistle especially. There are flashes of scarlet and spatterings of orange, but they are eye-catching exceptions to the rule. It would be tempting to think that the planting was haphazard, and yet it is not. Faith Raven's instinct has been to plant what she likes where she likes – and the result is delightful.

Mrs Raven and her late husband John bought the property in 1954 when the 1½-acre (0.6ha) garden contained little of any consequence except for a few fine trees. At the time John Raven had some small experience of gardening and had a passionate interest in British wild flora. Faith Raven's practical experience had been limited to a rooftop garden in her London home and a rocky prominence in the Western Highlands of Scotland, which she still manages.

The Ravens began working on the garden from the house outwards, so that their earliest plantings enhanced the view from the windows.

A strong framework of existing walls and planted hedges encloses or semi-encloses gravelled and paved courtyards and themed gardens, each with an individual character. A rectangular pond on a patio sheltered by a wall of one of the barns is marked at each corner by a clipped box cone in a large terracotta container – the closest this garden ever gets to geometric formality.

Other box cones of varying heights and sizes – tall, elegant ones and short, dumpy ones – punctuate herbaceous borders

without ever dominating or detracting from the Impressionist look.

The dryness of the climate at Shepreth and the quick-draining, gravelly and moderately alkaline soil proved ideal for Mediterranean plants. As each new area of the garden was taken into cultivation – a further 1 acre (0.4ha) of land has since been added – so the need for more plants grew. Faith Raven says that she increased her plant collection in those early days by securing cuttings, seedlings and established plants with 'magpie acquisitiveness' from friends and family, nursery gardens and plant-seeking expeditions abroad.

Her preference for species over hybrids and old-fashioned varieties as opposed to 'modern novelties', and the way they are allowed to intertwine and intermingle, gives all the borders a nostalgically cottage-garden look. Seedlings are allowed to grow wherever they sow themselves; bulbs and small clumps of herbs thrust through cobbles, gravel and cracks in paving; and roses are planted among herbaceous species and fruit trees, which they use as climbing frames.

Faith Raven uses tall perennials with inspirational effect. In one border the towering spires of *Eremurus himalaicus*, like thrusting white candles, dwarf even the tallest white and blue delphiniums. In complete contrast of form and scale, the underplanting is of *Crambe cordifolia* which has clouds of minute, fragrant white flowers above ground-covering mounds of crinkled dark-green leaves.

The huge purple, thistle-like cardoon heads (*Cynara cardunculus*) are echoed at a lower level by the round globes of *Allium christophii*, their silver-grey foliage making a perfect foil for the pinkish-purple blooms of *Gladiolus italicus*. Mingled with these statement plants there are clouds of feathery fennel and bronze fennel and a dense

underplanting of *Geranium* 'Jackman's Blue'. In the Gravel Courtyard, sea kale (*Crambe maritima*) forms a grey-blue background.

Lining the path to the greenhouse there is a similar colour theme. Here allium and fennel play supporting roles to some of Faith Raven's collection of long-established peonies in shades from near magenta to palest sugar-icing pink, cream and pure white. Cotton thistle (*Onopordum acanthium*) with its medium-sized purple flower heads reinforces the colour palette and adds height and structure. In other borders height and substance are provided by willow wigwams supporting densely flowering early clematis.

The highlight of the Temple Garden is a delightfully elegant gazebo, a gift from King's College, Cambridge, where John Raven was a Fellow. It has a brilliant turquoise dome, almost veiled in midsummer with *Rosa glauca*. This vigorous, arching species rose has fine, greyish-purple leaves and red stems. The small, five-petalled single flowers, cerise pink with pale centres and gold stamens, have the 'innocent' look of wild roses growing in the hedgerows.

This is a garden created for meandering through and lingering in. Visitors are invited to wander round at leisure, probe into corners and choose ideas for plant associations suitable for their own conditions. Take a notebook with you – Faith Raven's instinctive planting has noteworthy ideas for gardeners everywhere.

The village of Shepreth, mentioned in the Domesday Book, was a frequent resting place for livestock being moved north to the Cambridge market. The word 'shepreth' means 'a brook in which sheep are washed'. Docwra's Manor also has a connection with sheep farming and was a working farm until 1919 when the manor house and the land were divided. The original manor, which featured in 11th-

century records, took its name from a family from Docker Hall in Kendal, Cumberland, when several of them moved south to settle near the lucrative wool trade at the Stourbridge Fair in Cambridge. There is a brass rubbing *c*1520 commemorating a Lady Dockra, Kath Haseldon.

Although parts of the present manor house may date from the 15th-century agricultural revival, it is essentially an 18th-century red-brick house. The kitchen wing was originally a floored barn, probably used to store wool.

The house and some outbuildings are Grade II* and are under covenant to the National Trust.

Left: This cluster planting of orange hemerocallis and yellow verbascum is an exception; most other borders feature soft blue, pink, mauve and white colour themes

Below: The layered look, in stages from the white ground cover to the gleaming spires

DODDINGTON HALL
Lincolnshire LN6 4RU

5 miles (8km) west of Lincoln | Open Sun & BH mid-Feb to end Oct, plus Wed Easter to end Sep | Tel: 01522 694308 | www.doddingtonhall.com

The formal gardens that complement the magnificent 16th-century house are maintained so faithfully to the original Elizabethan layout that it is possible to lose oneself in a time warp. One could be walking into the setting of a costume drama. The mellow, turreted house is seen from many angles through soldierly rows of tall pyramidal and cylindrical topiary structures, architectural achievements in their own right.

The house was designed by architect Robert Smythson for Thomas Taylor, registrar to the Bishop of Lincoln, and has been passed from family to family ever since; never sold in over four centuries. Claire Birch, the present owner, is a descendant of George Jarvis who inherited the property in 1830.

Within the 5-acre (2ha) framework of the Elizabethan walls – the original courtyards

– are gardens that thrill from early spring to late autumn: formal parterres, sumptuous herbaceous borders, drifts of naturalised bulbs, scented shrubs, ancient trees and orchard fruits. Beyond the enclosing walls there is a 2-acre (0.8ha) Kitchen Garden, as productive as ever, a Wild Garden and a nature trail which wends for about 1 mile (1.6km) through woodland, open parkland and a wetland meadow.

Left: Make a date to see this glorious display on one of the Snowdrop Sundays

Below: 'World Premier' bearded iris, resplendent here in one of the parterres. Doddington Hall has specialised in bearded iris for more than 25 years

Right: The box-edged parterres create an elegant living tapestry

The West Garden, reorganised in 1900 with the help and advice of the Royal Botanic Gardens at Kew, encapsulates much of the drama. In April there are dozens of rare and elegant Edwardian daffodils along with naturalised orange and golden crown imperial lilies; later, in May, a large handkerchief tree, *Davidia involucrata*, a native of China, is coming into flower and the colour palette of the herbaceous borders

is strengthening all the time. White wisteria clads the walls, magnolia trees are in full flower and a fountain sparkles. But it is the tapestry of the box-edged parterres that has an even more spectacular quality. In late May and early June many of these enclosures, some rectangular, some curved, are massed with blocks of blue and mauve bearded iris, breathtakingly beautiful and a speciality of the Doddington gardens where they have been grown for 25 years. The parterres were once resplendent, as was the fashion of the times, with old-fashioned roses, which here succumbed to disease. Gradually, now, roses are being reintroduced to the parterres, the double yellow cupped flowers of the fragrant floribunda *Rosa* 'Arthur Bell' a charming foil to the neighbouring irises.

The herbaceous borders, luxuriantly wide, are lavishly planted with peonies and phlox, alliums and delphiniums and, providing added height, the rich golden flowers of *Telekia speciosa*.

The Wild Garden, developed over a period of 20 years, presents a spectacular pageant of spring bulbs beginning in February with snowdrops (check the website for Spring Bulb Sundays), swathes of pale-mauve *Crocus tommasinianus* and splashes of carmine-flowered *Cyclamen coum*. Successively through the season, aconites, dog's-tooth violets (*Erythronium dens-canis*), Lenten lilies, Victorian species of daffodils,

Left: Hebe the cup-bearer, serene and elegant in her rose-covered arbour

Right: An overview of the intriguing variety of designs carried out in the geometric parterres

pheasant's-eye narcissus and snake's head fritillaries are a painterly sight. Cow parsley dapples the long grass with its white confetti-like flowers, and fragrant shrubs, climbing roses, rhododendrons, sorbus and ancient contorted sweet chestnut trees compose a varied landscape.

Here in the Wild Garden Antony Jarvis, Claire Birch's father, built the classical Temple of the Winds in memory of his parents. In the 1980s he created a turf maze based on an ancient design at Alkborough in North Lincolnshire, which encourages children to 'hopscotch' every which way around it to reach the centre.

And especially for his grandchildren, and to intrigue and amaze other young visitors, Antony Jarvis hid what he called a 'dinosaur's egg' (a boulder) amid the branches of a field maple.

Time is of the essence when planning a visit to Doddington gardens. From the massed glories of the spring bulbs, through the majesty of the herbaceous borders and parterres in summer and on to the burnished leaf colour and berries of autumn, one is spoilt for choice.

EAST RUSTON GARDENS Norfolk NR12 9HN

1 mile (1.5km) south of Happisburgh | Open daily Easter to Oct | Tel: 01692 650432 | **www.eastrustonoldvicarage.co.uk**

Just a mile and a half from the Norfolk coast there is a garden that, defying the infamous East wind, takes one on an improbable horticultural tour. Protected now by belts of trees and cosseted by dense hedges there are gardens with the ambience of the Mediterranean, the luxuriance of the tropics, the aridity of the Arizona desert and, in a field spattered with cornflowers and poppies, the nostalgia of childhood.

This exhilarating complex of gardens is all the more wondrous because it rises out of an area given over to large-scale cereal farming where there is no longer any economical place for hedges, ditches and ponds.

Alan Gray and Graham Robeson bought the property in 1973 when the former vicarage had a look of desolation and the surrounding 2 acres (0.8ha) were waist high in weeds. They saw this as a chance for ambition and imagination to have free rein; a blank canvas on which to create an oasis-like cordon around the Arts and Crafts brick-and-tile house.

At first living and working in London, they were commuter gardeners until in the mid-1980s they moved in, pick, spade and shovel. Within a few years they were able to buy first one parcel and then another of the adjoining glebe land until now – they say this is the end

– the garden and woodlands extend over 32 acres (13ha).

To protect the tender, rare and unusual plants they grow and propagate the owners planted large shelter belts of Monterey pine (*Pinus radiata*), Italian alder (*Alnus cordata*), the Mediterranean oak, *Quercus ilex* and many eucalypts which, as they developed, improved the micro-climate. More protection comes from mixed hedgerows planted for their changing colours and textures and as habitats for birds and other wildlife.

Evergreen hedges, obelisks, blocks, balls and other decorative structures – even a pair of hornbeam 'houses' with pointed roofs and an archway – play a large part in the overall structure of the garden. Decorative they certainly are, but these hedges are wind-defying too. In a further attempt to cheat the wind, Gray and Robeson dug into a slope to create a deep, sun-trapping sunken garden with a square, water-filled basin displaying and reflecting a glass and stainless steel sculpture. Large blocks of yew add formality to an area almost hidden from view. This is now the Rose Garden, having been completely revamped in 2010.

It took excavation on an equally arduous scale to create the conditions needed to replicate the rapid drainage facility of the Arizona desert after its occasional rainfall. Layers and layers of gravel, the top one mixed with soil, and hundreds of tons of pebbles went into the preparation of the garden where now, in this East Anglian climate, agaves, aloes, puyas, beschorneria, dasylirion (bear grass) and many varieties of cactus flourish.

Brick walls that retain and reflect the heat cosset a series of south-facing terraces in the Mediterranean Garden where palms, grasses, agapanthus and kniphofia are almost put in the shade, metaphorically speaking, by 6-feet-long (2-metre) shrimp-pink curving stems of the Mexican *Beschorneria yuccoides* and the 12-feet-high (4-metre) pink- and white-flowering columns of *Echium pininana* from the Canary Islands.

Formal and natural-looking ponds have encouraged the return of wildlife that had long lost its local habitat. Minnows ripple the surface of one of the formal pools, newts, toads and frogs enliven the boundaries of a large natural-looking pond and fairy-like dragonflies and damselflies flutter and hover. Presenting the gardeners with the greatest

compliment of all, a pair of kingfishers has taken up residence.

Part of Gray and Robeson's vision was to maintain a high level of colour and interest for as long as possible, and to give the garden a sense of place by harnessing nearby landmarks. A porthole in a hedge neatly frames the Happisburgh lighthouse, and the parting between poplars at the end of the Apple Walk seems to enclose Happisburgh Church, which is over a mile away, within the confines of the garden.

The extended season of colour is nowhere better exemplified than in a field and woodland garden which, criss-crossed by meandering paths, has a naturalistic feel. Several thousand bulbs are planted each year to reinforce the already glorious display of snowdrops and aconites in February. The scene shifts markedly through the changing colours and textures of a collection of hydrangeas in summer before the golden gleam of autumn takes over with magnificently colourful trees including liquidambars and black gums (*Nyssa sylvatica*). It is a similar story in the Fern Garden where a dense canopy of tree ferns has an under-storey that progresses from pink and white hellebores and narcissi through pink hardy begonias to the rich blues of aconitum.

The Exotic Garden is awash with bedding plants, many not now available commercially but kept going by the owners' love of tall-growing tender plants like the salvias grown by our forebears. Bananas and *Tetrapanax papyrifer* 'Rex' add structure with their large imposing foliage and the tall fountain adds drama, splashing away on hot days.

A new Walled Garden is nearing completion called the '2012 Diamond Jubilee Walled Garden'. Here will be a traditional greenhouse with peach trees, tomatoes and

peppers and raised beds containing fruit, vegetables, flowers for cutting and much more, all designed to give pleasure to the eye as well as the soul, for here the planting will be traditional, but with a modern twist.

Perhaps the summer chiefly belongs to the (usually) red and purple border where, in a wooden summer house in the centre of a long ribbon of flowering plants, visitors can sit amongst a profusion of roses, alliums and dahlias; or to outlying fields-in-miniature planted with rows and rows of sun-worshipping sunflowers and shoulder-high sweetcorn. Forget Norfolk. This could be southern France.

The Winter Garden at East Ruston Old Vicarage has lessons every gardener can learn – colour, form and texture; and, uniquely, the view of Happisburgh lighthouse at the end of the walk.

Alan Gray and Graham Robeson have planned their winter wonderland by planting birches for their white, cream or rusty-red stems; dogwoods and willows for their red, gold and yellow stems; and hollies with leaves from deep green to variegated shades of yellow and cream and berries from scarlet through orange to gold. The spiky outlines of phormiums in various hues add architectural interest, and grasses that change from green to tan and cream have an ethereal quality. A group of eucalyptus trees with textural trunks in shades of cream, tan and grey makes a glistening background of foliage cover, the more so when the garden is touched by frost.

When planning for winter colour and interest, think leaf, bark and berry, these innovative gardeners advise, and you can't go wrong. 'As the years go by, the garden becomes our refuge from what appears to us to be an increasingly hostile world. We hope that visitors, too, may experience the joy and tranquillity of the garden.'

ELTON HALL Cambridgeshire PE8 6SH

11 miles (17.5km) west of Peterborough | **Open selected days Apr to Sep or by appointment** | **Tel: 01832 280468** | **www.eltonhall.com**

There has been a house where Elton Hall stands for nearly 550 years. The medieval buildings, which included the Tudor tower and chapel that remain, were surrounded by a moat and little else. In the 17th century a new house was built, the moat filled in and a small formal garden planted. A hundred years later the garden was expanded in a picturesque, formal manner and sketches show lawn, trees and a few shrubs. In the 1890s additional shrubberies and a box parterre were planted. Finally, in 1911, the garden was laid out much as you see it today. This Edwardian garden, which was designed to be tended by 13 gardeners, amounted to a total of 27 acres (11ha) and included the Walled Garden which has now become a Plant Centre. After World War II it became impossible for the estate to continue to manage a garden on such a scale and so the area was reduced and the number of gardeners cut to three.

By 1980 a large part of the garden had fallen into disrepair. The size of the garden was reduced again and some areas returned to parkland. The rest of the garden has since been enthusiastically restored. New hedges have formed intimate gardens which include a stunning Gothic orangery built to celebrate the millennium. Topiary parterres and immaculately kept lawns and paths give structure to many unusual plants.

In the middle of the Sunken Garden there is a lily pond surrounded by billowing borders, bright in summer with an unusual selection of flowering plants, among them *Papaver orientale* 'Mrs Perry', peonies, *Philadelphus* 'Manteau d'Hermine' with its fragrant creamy-white flowers, and *Crambe cordifolia*. Recently, a new flower garden was created from the former rose garden, which had suffered for many years with rose

sickness. These new borders are now well established and the mixture of herbaceous plants, grasses and shrubs has added wonderful colour and texture throughout the summer. A large spiral fountain in the centre echoes the towering pinnacles on the house.

The gardens are now maintained with two full-time gardeners, modern machinery and occasional extra help. A rigorous schedule of tasks keeps the hedges, plants and grass in check during the spring and summer months so that visitors may enjoy gardens that are in the Edwardian manner if not the scale.

Left: Millennium Orangery by Christopher Smallwood

Below: Flower forms decorate the scrolls in an intriguing niche in the Shell Grotto designed by Charlotte Kerr-Wilson

Right: Roses, sedums and salvias in the Flower Garden

HADDON HALL
Derbyshire DE45 1LA

2 miles (3km) south east of Bakewell | Open daily end Apr to end Oct | Tel: 01629 812855 | www.haddonhall.co.uk

Perched high above the River Wye on a limestone escarpment, Haddon Hall is one of the most romantic medieval castles in England. The grey and honey colour of its stonework is a sharp contrast to the rich green of the woodland behind, and beautiful gardens spill down in a series of walled terraces from Dorothy Vernon's door at the very top of the castle almost to the level of the river itself.

Legend has it that Haddon Hall came into the hands of the Dukes of Rutland when the Vernon heiress eloped with John Manners, son of the then Earl of Rutland, in 1558, running down the 76 drystone steps and across the packhorse bridge to meet her lover.

Whatever the truth of the story, the steps from Dorothy Vernon's door, which is the route by which the modern visitor leaves the house, descend to a terrace which was once a bowling alley. When the 9th Duke of Rutland restored Haddon in 1912, he cleared this terrace of giant yews and sycamores, as well as ivy on the walls. Pairs of clipped yew trees are again a feature of this garden which, in the spring, glows with more than 60 varieties of daffodil, polyanthus and wallflower. As summer approaches, the roses take over: first the climbers, then the floribundas and the hybrid teas in the formal beds. Haddon also boasts a collection of clematis, with 'Mrs Cholmondeley' showing large, blue blooms in early summer beside the upper door.

A wide flight of steps leads down to the Fountain Terrace which lies beneath the irregular window panes of the magnificent Elizabethan long gallery. A simple, rectangular pool with its delicate jet of water contrasts with the surrounding lawn and new wild flower area, enhanced by beech and hornbeam topiary, the design of Arne Maynard, a Chelsea Flower Show award winner. Wide borders are brimming with

delphiniums, lythrums, nepeta and shrub roses, their soft colours complementing the ancient stonework. The gallery wall itself is covered with a variety of climbing roses, threaded with clematis, lathyrus and ipomoea.

From the end of the Fountain Terrace there are spectacular views over the River Wye and the surrounding countryside. Every Friday throughout the summer season the lower terraces are open to the public. Sheltered niches in the buttressed walls house tender shrubs, and kiwi vines climb to great heights.

Left: Delphiniums in all their glorious painterly shades stand tall in the shelter of the house

Above: Topiary art enters the realms of fantasy!

Right: Clematis lines the pathway to the house

157

HELMINGHAM HALL Suffolk IP14 6EF

Helmingham Hall is the home of the ancient Tollemache family. Standing serenely inside its deep moat, the mellow brickwork of the Tudor house is appropriately surrounded by a magnificent garden centred on a 19th-century parterre. This is edged with a beautiful spring border which leads into a lushly planted enclosure on the site of the old kitchen garden. Beyond this again is an orchard and apple walk; on the other side of the house is a historical knot and herb garden designed in 1982 for the Tollemaches by Lady Salisbury.

Entering the main gardens along a grassy causeway which runs between the house moat and the one which surrounds the parterre, you come at once to a rose garden filled with hybrid musks. Here, the familiar 'Penelope', 'Felicia', 'Pink Prosperity' and 'Buff Beauty' bloom alongside rarer varieties such as 'Danae', 'Daybreak' and 'Nur Mahal'; there are also American roses such as 'Bishop Darlington'. This part of the garden is a wide rectangle with classical stone figures at each end, the banks dotted with primroses and narcissi in spring. The roses themselves grow in wide beds edged with Hidcote lavender and underplanted with London pride, which provides a carpet through which peonies, *Campanula lactiflora* and alstroemeria also grow.

Through the gates of the Walled Garden, a central grassy path divides the area into eight beds, as it did when this was an Elizabethan kitchen garden. Bordered by herbaceous plants and backed by climbing roses, among them 'Albertine' and 'New Dawn', the vegetable plots are divided by walks and arched tunnels on which sweet peas, gourds and runner beans grow.

The main herbaceous borders are immensely colourful with acanthus, alliums, delphiniums, achillea and *Papaver orientale*, while the Orchard Garden in spring is covered with primroses, cowslips, wild orchids and ox-eye daisies. The low box hedges of the Knot Garden to the east of the house contain a medley of herbs. There is also a magnificent collection of shrub roses mixed with campanulas, geraniums, foxgloves and lady's mantle (*Alchemilla mollis*). Enclosed by yew hedges, this is a beautiful garden where all the plants have been chosen to be contemporary with the house.

Left: The impressive façade of the Tudor mansion with the 'house moat' in the foreground

Above: Golden glory: a broad walk edged with immaculate topiary domes and wayward grasses streaked by autumn sunlight

HENSTEAD EXOTIC GARDEN Suffolk NR34 7LD

 5 miles (8km) south east of Beccles | Open by appointment | Tel: 01502 743006 | www.hensteadexoticgarden.co.uk

For centuries Andrew Brogan's 400-year-old cottage has been sheltering between a 10-foot-high (3-metre) yew hedge on the country lane and a 15-acre (6ha) ancient wood beyond the garden at the back. And so when in 2000 he moved from London to this Suffolk idyll, a favourable micro-climate was already established; up to a point, that is. Andrew planned to create a 'hardy exotic' garden in which all the plants – with the sole exception of a red ensete banana – would be left outside, without the protection even of a fleece, to survive the rigours of the fierce East-Anglian winters. Two recent, record-breakingly severe seasons were not, as Andrew puts it, for the faint-hearted, but his garden went into survival mode and largely fulfilled his hopes and – he adds – prayers.

What was not established when Andrew took over the garden was the necessary groundwork. The volume of rocks, stones and hardcore needed to create the foundation for his exotic garden was calculated in terms of tons – as many as 50. The volume of plants he has established since then is in high numbers too – 10 large tree ferns, *Dicksonia antarctica*, which grow 12 inches (30cm) every 10 years; 15 large bananas; 50 large palms including six different types, all growing in the ground unprotected; over 100 bamboos and countless yuccas, puyas and ferns.

With tiers of rocks, low stone walls and curved paths in place to give the garden the look he wanted, Andrew bought some large, well-established plants to get it off to a good start, moving the containerised plants around and changing their positions until he was satisfied with the overall effect of their relative heights and forms.

After this initial luxury of buying mature plants, he has taken a pride in propagating

from his stock. Twelve large clumps of the giant reed *Arundo donax* which produce 1-inch-thick (2.5cm) canes and spikelets of yellow flowers in summer and grow to a height of 13 feet (4 metres) started as one section of a plant he lifted from his London garden. Offshoots taken from his original Japanese banana plant have resulted in the 15 plants now developing in different parts of the garden. Others are given as presents to friends or sold on the plant stall on open days.

Andrew has recently extended the garden into part of the adjoining ancient woodland, which is full of huge oak, yew and holly trees. He pruned some of the lower branches to reveal what he describes as amazing over-100-year-old trunks going in all directions, a perfect backdrop to his cultivated garden. He feels that this harmonious juxtaposition of established natives and imported exotics will dispel the theory that never the twain shall meet.

A further and ongoing development, also a part of the newly colonised land, is the establishment of strictly working areas, including large compost bins, logs for fuel, wood for future buildings and finally – for now at least – a large polytunnel for propagating, potting on and looking after his huge stock of potted plants. Work has also started on a composting lavatory, which this innovative gardener describes as a 'lovely *Lord of the Rings*-style wooden building'.

Andrew notices that even in a relatively small garden such as this the micro-climate changes from one area to another; he also factors in the effect that certain plants will have on others.

A massive evergreen oak, for example, creates shade and a dry environment that is favourable to echiums and cordylines. The poor soil in some parts of the garden can be a positive advantage.

Left: Moisture-loving plants hug the poolside with its 'sunray' island crossing

Above: Strikingly contrasting leaf shapes – and their translucence – contribute to the lush appearance of this exciting symphony in greens and reds

A small lomatia tree would die if he fed it or moved it to a better place. He does not have a greenhouse and does not mollycoddle his plants, even by covering them with fleece. The resilience of so many plants has surprised him, and he says that most look equally good in baking sunshine or a light covering of snow.

Not all the plants in the garden would be termed exotic. Andrew's philosophy is that if a shrub or other flowering plant survives and looks good, then it should be given a chance. Thus there are clumps of pink and crimson bergenias growing beneath tree ferns. A waterfall that tumbles over jagged rocks is flanked by an eclectic mix of moisture-loving ferns and giant gunnera, canna lilies, foxgloves and kniphofia, and large fan-shaped palms that display their leaves as if they were peacock tails.

Two garden buildings invaded on all sides by gunnera and bamboo have already lost the appearance of being newcomers. One Andrew describes as being like a gingerbread house, the other, on stilts, is a Thai-style shelter with a scooped roof and long benches, a perfect viewing pavilion especially when the garden is softly lit in the evening.

Three large ponds, one stocked with koi carp and golden orfe, attract dragonflies; on a good day (or evening) they will fly around the garden in droves. Pheasants strut around the garden as if it were their own, their red, green and blue plumage a camouflage against the colourful foliage. Bananas ripen, if slowly, and plants from as far away as New Zealand, the Himalayas and Japan flourish.

It is the Suffolk country cottage with its Gothic-style door and windows that seems to belong to a far-off land.

HODSOCK PRIORY
Nottinghamshire S81 0TY

2 miles (3km) south west of Blyth | Open daily for 4 weeks Feb to Mar; check dates | Tel: 01909 591204 | **www.snowdrops.co.uk**

For those who like to tread the path of history and – suitably wrapped up – enjoy a winter wonderland walk, Hodsock Priory, on the Nottinghamshire–Yorkshire border, is an absolute must.

The estate was mentioned in the Domesday Book – although its occupation far predates that time – when it was stated that it 'had 2 carucates of land taxable', a carucate being 120 acres (48.5ha). For over 200 years from the mid-12th century the property was owned by the powerful Cressey family who, over time, entertained three kings, Henry II, John and Edward I; and in 1541 King Henry VIII was entertained there.

The sturdy, impressive Grade I-listed gatehouse dates from 1485. The adjacent red-brick house and the Italianate terrace were built partly by the early Gothic Revivalist architect Ambrose Poynter in 1837, and in 1874 the remainder was rebuilt to a design by George Devey to complement the earlier buildings. The gardens were laid out under the direction of head gardener Arthur Ford early in the 20th century.

During World War II, Ford's gardens, which included a Fan Garden and separate walled kitchen gardens, were ploughed up for the production of vegetables by the Women's Land Army who were billeted in the house.

The property has been owned since 1765 by the Mellish family of Blyth Hall, from whom the Buchanans are descended, and it is now the home of George and Katharine Buchanan. It was George Buchanan's parents, Sir Andrew and Lady Buchanan, who laid the foundations for the snowdrop extravaganza when, having found a wealth of wild bulbs in the woodlands, they decided to boost their numbers with mass planting and to supplement the native trees with more beeches.

Consequently, for the past two decades Hodsock Priory has become increasingly renowned for the millions – literally – of snowdrops that cluster in the borders and cloak the woodlands and stream banks, ravishingly complemented by myriad other spring bulbs and flowering shrubs.

Now the snowdrop trail meanders through a clearly indicated 1-mile-long (0.6km) network of gravel, grass and bark paths, across bridges, over streams, around ponds and past the ancient moat; and everywhere there are carpets of snowdrops, some sandwiched between ribbons of one of the earliest-flowering daffodils, *Narcissus* 'Tête-à-Tête'. The Buchanans have become used to seeing visitors lying on paths to photograph or closely examine individual flowers.

Although doubtless they are the main attraction, the snowdrops are not the only reason to visit the 5-acre (2ha) Hodsock Priory garden, much of which has been restored to its pre-war character with a planted terrace, herbaceous borders and a bog garden as well as the ponds.

There are Victorian-style hives in the apiary (now fully restored after devastating damage from a fallen tree); the colourful stems of cornus and acers, white, green, blue, orange and red; the romantic fragrance of winter-flowering honeysuckle and sarcococca, Christmas or sweet box; banks of hellebores in all their subtle shades from

white and cream through to deep blues and purples; sun-bright yellow aconites and sky-blue iris; and the sense that, although introduced, these species have graced Hodsock for centuries.

Left: Ribbons of glorious *Narcissus* 'Tête-à-Tête' beautify the ancient moat

Below left: The snowdrop season is soon followed by a hazy blue undercarpet as thick ribbons of bluebells weave through the woodlands

Below: Gradually the snowdrops give way to other spring bulbs and flowering shrubs

ILMINGTON MANOR Warwickshire CV36 4LA

4 miles (6.5km) north west of Shipton-on-Stour | Open for NGS or by appointment | Tel: 01608 682230 | www.ngs.org.uk

Few who visit the lovely 3-acre (1.2ha) gardens of Ilmington Manor today would guess that they are mainly only 90 years old. When the late Mr and Mrs Spenser Flower came to this delightful village in 1919, the honey-coloured stone manor house, built by Sir Thomas Andrews and dating from 1600, needed massive restoration, and an orchard occupied the position of the present garden. With a flair for design and with a clear idea of what they wanted, the Flowers restored and enlarged the manor house, planted many specimen trees and set about creating the interesting and beautiful flower- and topiary-filled gardens that we see today. Their grandson, Martin Taylor, is the present owner who, with his late wife Miranda, completed the restoration of the manor and its cottages and gardens.

To the right of the drive, which is lined with hornbeams, is a little yew-hedge-bordered Pond Garden. The edges of the square pond are decorated with carved stone panels from India and the surrounding paving is overgrown with many different varieties of scented thyme. The beds are filled with pink diascia, dianthus and other sun-lovers, while trailing sedums continue the patterns on the walls of the pool. This attractive area is bounded to the north and east by walls draped with clematis, a fine banksia rose and other aromatic climbers, but it is a surprise to find *Buddleia crispa*, as this has a reputation for tenderness.

Beyond the forecourt, to the south of the house, are three large walnut trees and a dovecote perched high above a neatly clipped hedge; drifts of naturalised daffodils

Above: On a large lawn just behind this intimate area of the garden there are two large chess-piece-like topiary forms – now slightly tilted with age – flanked by low stone walls

Above right: A touch of gold among drifts of tall shrubs

Right: Beautiful old stone walls, pillars and steps enhance the garden at every turn

and brightly coloured crocuses enliven the area in spring.

To the west of the house, steps lead into the large formal Rose Garden, planted with old and modern shrub roses. Contributing to the exquisite beauty of this area are 'Madame Hardy' and 'Scarlet Fire' as well as 'Louise Odier', 'Cerise Bouquet' and 'Charles de Mills', together with 'Alex Red', 'Arthur Bell', 'Scented Air' and 'Just Joey'.

The so-called Cupid Garden – really more of an informal cottage garden – is one of the most colourful parts of Ilmington Manor. Designed by the present owner's late wife Miranda, it features the most enchanting mixture of roses, lavender and scented mock oranges, with peonies and hardy geraniums standing alongside clematis-clad walls. Nearby is Miranda's Buddha, a white garden walk with white camellia and white roses and hellebores.

The Long Walk has six well-stocked herbaceous borders that form the centrepiece of the main garden. Ilmington Manor gardens are a haven of peace and beauty in all seasons.

MANNINGTON HALL Norfolk NR11 7BB

18 miles (29km) north west of Norwich | Open selected days May to Sep; times vary | Tel: 01263 768444 | www.manningtongardens.co.uk

Only 7 miles (11km) from the sea in the open, rolling countryside of north Norfolk is the romantic Mannington Hall. Purchased in the 18th century by Horatio, the first Lord Walpole, brother of Sir Robert Walpole, the lovely medieval moated house is still owned by that family. There are a number of richly contrasting areas to interest the garden-lover, especially the Heritage Rose Garden – a deliciously scented layout – and, near the entrance, an arboretum planted with native trees.

Walking across the spacious lawns towards the house, it is clear that storms have damaged some of the great cedars, but fast-growing new cedars and wellingtonias have been planted to replace those that were lost. Inside the Victorian 'battlement' walls, the borders are overflowing with herbaceous plants and roses, notably with *Rosa* 'Canary Bird' showing its single yellow blooms in late spring. The bed beneath the house wall has peonies and lupins. A fine climbing hydrangea, *H. petiolaris*, cloaks the wall and opposite is a splendid weeping pear with grey-green leaves.

Far left: A pergola covered with *Rosa* 'Rambling Rector'

Left: *Rosa* 'Harry Maasz' and *R.* 'Mozart'

Above: Drawbridge flanked by *Centranthus ruber*

Around the corner of the house *Rosa banksiae* 'Lutea', the yellow banksian rose, climbs vigorously close to a mauve wisteria, while other low-growing shrubs brighten up the gravel with their pink and white flowers in early summer. A formal rose garden dominated by hybrid teas and with a sundial in the centre is surrounded by juniper. Within the moat sweetly scented herbs in an intricate pattern in the form of the Hall's dining-room ceiling are planted underneath urns filled with hyacinths in spring and then replaced by various scented plants.

Fruit trees line the intimate enclosure of the Heritage Rose Garden, which is divided into several areas, each representing a period of the rose's historical development. In all there are more than 1,000 different varieties, including a wide range of species roses. The Medieval Garden has turf seats and some very old roses, including *Rosa gallica officinalis* and *R. spinosissima* which stand near a small yew tree. Other formal areas of Mannington Hall include a tranquil 17th-century knot garden. Across the road from the Hall, in a totally different mood, is the ruined church in a wild valley with many fascinating and unusual trees, including specimens of *Acer palmatum* which are well over 100 years old.

Newer developments are a sensory garden with plants selected for sound, smell and taste as well as appearance; an area for the less able with shaded seats and raised beds; and a 'hot' area with Mediterranean plants.

MOSELEY OLD HALL

In one of the less promising parts of Wolverhampton you suddenly come upon the truly remarkable Moseley Old Hall, set in its equally amazing garden. From the outside, the house belies its age, but as soon as you enter it is clear that this is a timber-framed Tudor manor house – and indeed, it is the building in which the future Charles II took refuge after his defeat at the Battle of Worcester in 1651. When the property was given to the National Trust in 1962 it was in a poor condition, and the 1-acre (0.5ha) garden was virtually non-existent. Within a very short time, however, Graham Stuart Thomas, assisted by Miles Hadfield, had recreated the garden in the mid-17th-century style which, now fully matured, forms the wonderful layout we see today.

The main feature of the garden is the knot which lies to the south of the Hall and is best seen from its upper windows. A copy of one designed by the Reverend Walter Stonehouse in 1640, it consists of 11 clipped spheres of box standing on 3-foot (1m) sterns surrounded by circular gravel beds edged with dwarf box hedges. Along one side of the knot is an arbour now draped with the fragrant *Clematis flammula*, the white-flowering virgin's bower, and *C. viticella*, making a contrast with the deep-purple teinturier grape, while narrow borders are filled with strongly scented lavender.

The arbour leads through a hornbeam tunnel to the Nut Alley, lined on each side with different varieties of snowdrop, winter aconite and the Siberian squill flower in early spring. These are succeeded by the stinking hellebores and by snake's-head fritillary, followed in autumn by colchicums and pink-flowering cyclamens. At the end of the alley is the gate through which Charles Stuart is supposed to have entered secretly, and in the field beyond is one sweet chestnut, all that remains from the Long Walk. The flagged path leading to the back door is lined with morello cherries, quinces, black mulberries and medlars. At the far end is a small herb garden enclosed by box, with a fragrant mock orange underplanted with Lenten roses.

The front garden, once a paved court, now consists of lawns with spirals and cones of *Lonicera nitida* and holly, and two beds of tutsan edged by *Teucrium chamaedrys*. The mixed borders against the walls are filled with splendid herbs including Solomon's seal, red valerian, the pink and white varieties of *Paeonia officinalis*, and the lovely garden herb soapwort, the soapy sap of which is nowadays used in museums for laundering and revitalising precious fabrics.

Moseley Old Hall is an enchanting garden, full of interesting plants that were once grown to provide dyes and for medicinal and cleaning purposes and now contribute significantly to the ambience of this history-rich property.

Above: View down the path and through the timber arbour in the garden

Right: A view over the Knot Garden, a copy of a 17th-century design, with dwarf box trees standing in 11 spheres

7 miles (11.25km) south east of Bury St Edmunds | Open May to Sep only by appointment | Tel: 01359 270452 after 11am

Set deep in the Suffolk countryside near Bury St Edmunds is a small but distinguished herb garden, Netherfield Herbs. The owner, Lesley Bremness, has been growing herbs and writing about them now for more than 30 years, and a visit to Netherfield undoubtedly deepens one's knowledge about the many uses to which herbs can be put – in cooking, medicinal remedies, cosmetics and more. Lesley has found over the past four decades that the most valuable aspect of her herb garden is simply sitting among the herbs as, for her, this reduces stress, restores balance and can eventually recharge the mind with creative zest.

Beyond the 16th-century thatched cottage an arch in the yew hedge invites visitors to step into the herb garden and relax on a seat beneath an arbour covered with roses, hops and the hardy, semi-evergreen traditional Chinese herb *Akebia quinata*. This is an elegant climber with deliciously fragrant small, purple-red flowers and edible fruits. Nearby is the small-leaved sweet briar rose, Shakespeare's 'eglantine', whose apple-scented leaf fragrance is released in hot sun and after rain.

Four central diamond beds are devoted to varieties of sage, rosemary, oregano, marjoram and thyme. Marking two points of the diamond are a pair of large ball-shaped bay trees. Each has several close vertical stems as Lesley has found that bay trees with multiple stems are less likely to die in harsh winters. There is also a gold-variegated bay which seems to be more hardy than the green version.

Left: The old cottage is surrounded by trees, with *Rosa* 'Old Blush' in the foreground

Right: A contented cat dozes on a bench overhung with climbing rose 'New Dawn'

Another bed contains medieval salad herbs including smallage (*Apium graveolens*), an escapee from the ancient Abbey herb garden in Bury St Edmunds, the garlic-flavoured Jack-by-the-hedge and wild rocket, while the next bed has ancient medicinal herbs including feverfew, dwarf comfrey and the blood-cleansing tonic figwort (*Scrophularia nodosa*). Among the many culinary herbs are sweet cicely, tansy, broad-leaved sorrel and alecost or bible herb (*Tanacetum balsamita*) whose minty leaf was used as a book mark to help the laity stay awake through long sermons.

Amongst the cosmetic herbs, the soothing muscilage of marsh mallow (*Althaea officinalis*) has long been used externally in creams to treat weather-damaged skin and internally to soothe coughs and gastric ulcers. Similarly soothing is the rare Suffolk white-flowered form of musk mallow (*Malva moschata*): its young shoots are steamed and eaten to provide vitamins A, B and C and the flowers can adorn salads. Enchantingly, a small statue of Pan is embraced by the fragrant pink Apothecary's rose, *Rosa gallica officinalis,* with its culinary, medicinal, cosmetic and perfume uses.

In a wild corner outside the formal herb garden, the huge leaves of elecampane (*Inula helenium*) give a tropical jungle appearance – its aromatic root, said to have been the object of Helen of Troy's harvesting when she was abducted by Paris, was among the first medicinal sweets. Steamed roots were sliced and fried (changing the carbohydrates to sugars), giving a medicinal treat for those with difficult breathing.

The garden's newest additions are two standing stones, one a 9-foot (3-metre) stone of Welsh slate named the 'Star Stone', a gift from Lesley's four sons, with the intention that each son will add one for his family and then one for each new child, creating a fractal pattern of mini circles. By contrast, from 'Through the Moongate', the Chinese garden Lesley designed for the 2007 Chelsea Flower Show, Netherfield garden has a marble stone taken from the famous Tai Lake in China, where soft stones are submerged under water for 100 years and then moulded into fantastical shapes.

This most delightful garden which does so much to further the visitor's knowledge about herbal plants also gives aesthetic pleasure with its textures, scent and beauty.

NEWSTEAD ABBEY
Nottinghamshire NG15 8NA

11 miles (17.5km) north of Nottingham | Usually open daily | Tel: 01623 455900 | www.newsteadabbey.org.uk

Newstead Abbey has a long and distinguished history in which its gardens play an important part. Founded by Henry II as an Augustinian priory in the 12th century, Newstead was given to Sir John Byron of Colwick by Henry VIII in 1539, at the time of the dissolution of the monasteries. The 5th Lord Byron (1722–98) was responsible for adding the Upper Lake to the 25 acres (10ha) of gardens, but it is perhaps for its connection with his great-nephew, 19th-century poet the 6th Lord Byron, that the property, his childhood home, is best known. In 1798 at the age of ten, when he had

just inherited the title, he planted an oak, Byron's Oak, which now survives only as an ivy-covered stump; a young oak has been planted beside it. Byron sold Newstead in 1818 to his friend Thomas Wildman, a Jamaican plantation owner. His *Lines on Leaving Newstead Abbey* poignantly record the time when the property passed out of his family's ownership. Newstead came under the control of the Nottinghamshire County Council on presentation by the last owner, Sir Julian Cain, in the 1930s.

From the entry to the 300-acre (120ha) estate alongside the so-called Gospel Oak,

the long drive sweeps through rhododendron plantations that date from the 19th century, and crosses open heathland covered with heather to reach a car park to the north of the abbey. Water flows over a cascade into the Garden Lake, and the walls of the house are festooned with jasmine and the fragrant yellow rose 'Golden Showers'.

Close to the east wall is the Spanish Garden, so named because of an Iberian well head which is its centrepiece. This gives on to a gravel path bounded by a wall covered with hydrangeas and honeysuckles, its border filled with shade-

loving plants. A pocket handkerchief tree marks the entry to a dark tunnel which leads to Eagle Pond, one of the monks' original stew ponds (fishponds). Just to the west is the famous memorial to Boatswain, Byron's dog, and the wood beyond is planted with snowdrops and daffodils which make a brave, bright show in spring.

Beds at each end of the former Kitchen Garden display old-fashioned roses, while modern roses are set in beds surrounded by lawns; climbers and ramblers adorn the walls of the enclosure. Beyond the great Yew Walk is a fine rock garden and also the famous Japanese Garden commissioned by Miss Ethel Webb, whose family owned Newstead in the early years of the 20th century. Humpbacked bridges and stepping stones across the streams lead between rhododendrons, azaleas, mahonias, skimmias and bamboo. Returning to the Garden Lake, you can enjoy the beauty of a pergola covered with roses and other climbers, and what is probably the best view of the Abbey in this extensive and beautiful garden.

From *Lines on Leaving Newstead Abbey* by Lord Byron:

'Through thy battlements, Newstead,
    the hollow winds whistle,
Thou, the hall of my fathers, art gone
    to decay;
In thy once smiling garden, the hemlock
    and thistle
Have choked up the rose which late
    bloomed in the way...'

Left: The Spanish Garden

Top right: One of four wire sculptures by one-time artist-in-residence Derek Kinzett in the walled rose garden. The sculptures represent the 400 gardeners employed here in Lord Byron's time

Right: The man-made waterfall at Newstead Abbey

WOODCHIPPINGS

3 miles (5km) south of Brackley | Open Feb to mid-Jul by appointment | Tel: 01869 810170 | **www.ngs.org.uk**

This is a garden for all seasons, from January and February when the woodland is carpeted with the showy dark-carmine flowers of *Cyclamen coum*, with snowdrops and hellebores – prettiest of all when they are spattered with snow – through springtime when cherry trees scatter their pink blossom over grape hyacinth and the pink near-trumpet-shaped corydalis flowers. And then in summer when the beds and borders are packed with grasses and bright perennials, they have plant-lovers fast-scribbling names, colours and planting schemes.

Woodchippings is a plantsman's garden, owned and cared for by Valerie Bexley and Richard Bashford. It has been created on the site of an old orchard, one surely known to the characters in Flora Thompson's *Lark Rise to Candleford* which was set in the small hamlet of Juniper Hill. Some of the old plum trees survive to provide springtime colour, shade and sometimes fruit. And the essence of a true cottage garden lives on, the beds and borders a-tumble with densely planted species grown for their colour and scent and their insect-attracting properties.

Hellebores are one of Richard Bashford's passions and the garden is enhanced by many hybrid forms grown from the seed strain he develops. Spanning all the velvety colours from primrose yellow through softest pink to duskiest purple, they are all named *Helleborus x hybridus* 'Juniper Hill', in tribute to the name of the hamlet.

For all the skilful planting and expert handling, this is a casual garden, clearly labour-intensive yet delightfully lacking in formality. Both the woodland and the intensely planted borders closer to the cottage look so natural that they might just have 'happened'.

Statues are positioned here and there throughout the garden in an informal way too, with no attempt – even though one does resemble a Roman god – at classical placement. Some statues, a stone figure of a girl carrying a sheaf of wheat for example, might have just paused for thought wherever they happened to be. A boy piper nestling against an ivy-covered hedge might have chosen the perfect place to stop – he is the focal point at the end of a pathway. A stone urn giving height and form to a densely planted flower bed is encased in cascading branches of the English leander group rose 'Teasing Georgia', so enwrapped in the profusion of soft yellow flowers that they seem to emanate from the single container.

Metal arches, wooden pergolas and some tree trunks are shrouded in clematis and climbing roses, vertical planting that takes colour and interest to eye level and above. *Clematis* 'Rhapsody,' one of the first to flower, carries large sky-blue flowers skywards, and a cabin/studio is all but concealed behind a strong pinky-red clematis and the glorious *Rosa gallica* 'Belle Sans Flatterie'.

The wide borders around the cottage are painterly, irresistible in their gloriously uninhibited use of colour. Tall spikes of terracotta verbascum (mullein), kniphofia and blue and white delphiniums tower above purple alliums and pink-frilled Oriental poppies. Large clusters of day lilies, another of Richard Bashford's passions, have a long flowering season and give continuity to beds where other species come and go. A pathway through the orchard is delightfully encroached in summer by delicate, wild-looking single and double meconopsis, their yellow and orange flowers like beacons in the dappled light. And in June the collection of romantic old roses, many of them French, spread an aura of romance throughout the garden.

Woodchippings is one of several cottages nestling along a country lane, each tantalisingly obscured behind a tall hedge; this one is the farthest from the road. Go

Left: A modern sculpture adds a sense of movement to the old orchard in spring

Above: *Papaver orientale* **'Forncett Summer'**

in through a small wooden gate and be prepared to fall in love with this delightful country cottage garden.

Richard Bashford's displays of sun-loving hemerocallis, day lilies, in his Northamptonshire garden are inspirational. Among his sensational collection there are *Hemerocallis* 'Coburg Fright Wig', a delectable shade of apricot going on peach; *H.* 'Spanish Harlem', a fiesta-shade of magenta with golden spots; *H.* 'Janice Brown', with pale- to deep-pink petals; and *H.* 'Lilting Lavender', its outward-curling mauve petals flashed gold at the centres; showing that there are day lilies to suggest or complement any garden scheme.

Given favourable conditions, day lilies should flower until late summer. They thrive in a warm position in the garden, preferably in full sun, or at least in semi-shade. They like a moisture-retentive but not waterlogged soil. You can divide the rhizomes at any time, but it is best to plant them between

March and May. If they are planted later in the year they must be well watered throughout the summer.

In her book *Lark Rise to Candleford* Flora Thompson describes the energy and enthusiasm put into gardening at Juniper Hill at the beginning of the last century.

'The energy they brought to their gardening after a hard day's work in the fields was marvellous… Often, on moonlight nights in spring, the solitary fork of some one who had not been able to tear himself away would be heard and the scent of his twitch fire smoke would float in at the windows. It was pleasant, too, in summer twilight, perhaps in hot weather when water was scarce, to hear the *swish* of water on parched earth in a garden – water which had been fetched from the brook a quarter of a mile distant. "It's no good stintin' th' land," they would say. "If you wants anything out you've got to put summat in, if 'tis only elbow-grease."'

WYKEN HALL Suffolk IP31 2DW

8 miles (13km) north east of Bury St Edmunds | Open afternoons Apr to end Sep | Tel: 01359 250287 | www.wykenvineyards.co.uk

Left: The house and garden enclosures viewed from the hot border containing euphorbia, kniphofia and alliums with woven willow frames to support plants

Right: Yew hedge with archway of roses leading into a formal garden where a peacock struts his stuff

On an estate once occupied by the Romans, mentioned in the Domesday Book and now at the heart of a working farm, Wyken Hall is a half-timbered medieval manor house with multiple gables, banks of octagonal brick chimneys and an almost indefinable roof line. The garden, which was redesigned in the 1980s mainly by the owners, Sir Kenneth and Lady Carlisle, is a plant-lover's cameo framed by the Suffolk countryside. Plant colours vary from verdant to vibrant and the mood changes from restrained to wild in areas that blend seamlessly into the surrounding meadows and woodland.

The approach to the house strikes a formal note of introduction with a group of five circular box hedges laid out in the shape of a quincunx. One encloses a sparkling blue and white fountain made and fired by Clive Davies, a Suffolk potter. Others encircle elegant, tiered topiary sculptures quaintly reminiscent of chess pieces. In spring the box circles are highlighted by rings of crisp white tulips peeping through deep-blue forget-me-nots whilst in summer the bulbs give way to flowering herbs.

The higgledy-piggledy shape of the house, painted in the traditional terracotta 'Suffolk pink', has inspired the creation of 'secret' knot gardens that nestle in its sheltering hollows. These outside designer rooms, snugly protected by the warm terracotta walls, are further examples of the versatility of topiary. There are no two alike.

Low, clipped diamond-shaped box hedges corner-touch square parterres, and sculptural pyramids, cubes and spheres are planted as focal points. There are many permutations. A herb garden designed by Arabella Lennox-Boyd integrates with the knot garden, bringing together evergreen and annual herbs that would have propagated and self-seeded on this Suffolk land for centuries. Colour is used sparingly yet strikingly, with purple and gold predominating. Purple chives partner the golden marjoram that circles the sundial; orange-gold bearded irises team with purple *Allium christophii* and aquilegia in a bed that commands attention beside a further topiary garden; and violet-flowered abutilon meanders over the mellow walls of the house.

In early summer the scent of the rose garden extends way beyond its boundaries. Bordered on three sides by a hornbeam hedge and decorated with a long, flower-spattered pergola, this romantic area of the garden has been created around an old church font and planted with a collection of old-fashioned roses: deep magenta, softest lavender and palest sugar-almond pink, rich buttery yellow, pale apricot and only-just-cream – beautiful, blowsy and many-petalled blooms. It is pure, sensual, perfumed delight.

This is a garden for strolling, admiring, pondering and – the owners have ensured – sitting. Four blue-painted rocking chairs invite quiet reflection around a lavender hedge – the perfect way to appreciate environmental fragrance. A single chair is half-hidden amongst more lavender and softly brushed by a cascade of rambling roses and overhanging branches of apples. A Gothic-style bench encourages one to linger beside the herb-ringed sundial. An ogee-arched 'throne' seat, nestling beneath a yew hedge, is set in isolation amongst more tumbling herbs.

And then there is the pond. Through a gate and over to a natural pond, bounded by rushes and irises and floating with water lilies, there is a sturdy decking promontory furnished with – who could resist them? – a pair of Adirondack chairs.

In autumn when the woodland leaves are russet and gold, a 'hot bed' beside the kitchen garden wall is aflame too. Fiery red and orange dahlias predominate, their vibrancy echoed by towering kniphofia, heleniums and the dramatic, scarlet outlines of redwood stems. The challenging copper beech maze is at its most vibrant then, and squirrels scamper around the gazebo in the Nuttery.

There is a woodland walk to the south-facing vineyard, planted in 1988 and now producing award-winning wines. Chickens strut in the orchard and have decorative houses of their own. Peacocks jump down from the trees and are liable to greet visitors here, there and everywhere. Llamas roam the fields. So much to see, so much to inspire, in a garden designed to delight all the senses.

The pairing of golden-orange bearded iris and purple *Allium christophii* makes an exceptionally strong impact against the dark-green clipped hedges of the Wyken Hall Knot Garden. They are ideal 'plant partners' because of their contrasting colours, textures and forms. Iris grown from rhizomes and allium from bulbs both enjoy fairly rich, slightly alkaline and well-drained soil and a position in full sun.

To achieve a similar effect, plant rhizomes and bulbs in autumn or early spring. Increase your 'show' by dividing them in autumn or spring the following year, or by pulling away any off-sets they have produced, and plant them in the ground or in pots. Rhizomes and bulbs propagated in this way will flower

one or two years earlier than those grown from seed.

Allium produce seedheads that are almost as beautiful as the purple flowers and you may choose to leave these starry globes to dry on their tall, erect stems. Remember to cut the stems off close to ground level before the next flowering season.

NORTHERN ENGLAND | 5

Students of garden history will find much to interest them in the country gardens of Northern England. Here are two fine examples of Elizabethan knot gardens; some of the oldest and certainly the most fanciful topiary structures of all time; the oldest, and among the longest, pair of twin herbaceous borders in the country; glorious Capability Brown parkland with, now, a reconstructed walled garden designed by Piet Oudolf; and, in so many gardens, inspired, imaginative planting that is history in the making.

One of the few remaining landed estates in Cheshire, Arley Hall has been owned by Lord Ashbrook's family since the 12th century and they built their first house there in 1469. Nothing now remains of that building except the tithe barn, and the present house dates from 1840. The gardens, too, are remarkable, as records show that when Sir Peter and Lady Elizabeth Warburton lived at Arley in the 1740s, they created walled gardens, walks and shrubberies.

What the visitor sees today is the layout of intimate enclosures mainly established by Rowland and Mary Egerton-Warburton within the earlier brick walls in the 1840s, and now covering 12 acres (5ha).

The gardens are approached along an avenue of pleached limes and entered beneath the 19th-century clock tower. Around the corner of the tithe barn is the Flag Garden, named after the flagstones that surround the formal beds of floribunda roses edged by dwarf lavender. The brick walls that enclose it on two sides are covered with honeysuckles, hydrangeas and the flame creeper. Nearby is the Furlong Walk. As you pass along this elevated terrace you come to a break in the shrub borders which permits entry to Arley Hall's greatest feature, the double herbaceous border. The oldest in the country, for they are shown on a map of 1846, these borders are 90 yards (82 metres) long and flank a wide grass path, one side being backed by a brick wall and the other by a yew hedge.

Separated by huge buttresses of yew, the plants early in the season are quite restrained, confined to a palette of blues, mauves, yellow and white, but in summer the borders erupt into a kaleidoscope of fabulous colour.

Through an archway in the yew hedge are the Tea Cottage and lawns, with beds of shrub and species roses underplanted with geraniums. To the west is the famous Ilex Avenue – clipped holm oaks that were planted in the 1850s.

Close to the avenue is the Fish Garden, set with small conifers and two Japanese cherries; at its end, steps lead down to the Sundial Circle, with borders containing the shrub rose 'Erfurt' backed by azaleas, kalmias, cistus and philadelphus.

The Rootery is now planted with pieris, azaleas and rhododendrons, and in The Rough naturalised bulbs give a bold show in spring. The entrance to the Walled Garden is festooned with honeysuckle, and a lily pond is guarded by four Dawyck beeches.

Back towards the Flag Garden is the Herb Garden; mints, thyme, marjorams and bergamots flourish. The Scented Garden is filled with fragrant flowers all year round.

Left: Roses ramble and tumble around an urn encircled by nepeta

Below: The Walled Garden with its kaleidoscope of summer colour

When in the 1860s Charles Thellusson built a mansion on his 8,000-acre (3,240ha) South Yorkshire estate, the gardens were laid out in a 'high Victorian' formal Italianate style complementing the architecture of the house. Clipped box, yew and holly were established to form domed, pyramidal and cubic shapes, hedges and edges, and a marble fountain and a wealth of Italian statues were installed. One of the most romantic of these is a statue of Psyche holding a butterfly, the symbol of the soul.

Flights of steps leading from the terrace down to the extensive lawn were designed with extreme formality, with shallow urns at the head and marble greyhounds at the foot – though it was for horse racing and yachting that the wealthy Thellusson family was best known. Symmetrical flower beds, in keeping with the overall geometry of the design, are cut out of the turf, and in one of these a striking central feature, a three-tier Italian marble dolphin fountain, has been expertly restored to working order after years of inactivity.

Separate areas of the garden are linked by walks that formed part of the original concept, lined with clipped and shaped hedges and appearing all the more formal because of the statuary displayed at intervals. A box hedge outlines the Rose Garden where there are over 100 historic rose varieties, many of them 19th-century Portland roses, and where in May and June the air is heady with their perfume.

A restored iron pergola provides a romantic walkway through the Rose Garden, the stylised design of which was based on the shape of a rose leaf. Close to this original rose enclosure, a new collection of species roses has been planted, presenting a tapestry of vivid colour.

The Rock Garden, established in a quarry and benefiting from a micro-climate, has

Left: The three-tier marble dolphin fountain at the heart of symmetrical flower beds

Above: A pathway through the Rose Garden

been replanted as a fern dell, with some 70 known types of fern and more than 30 yet to be identified, reflecting and respecting the Victorian passion for these plants, known as pteridomania. The outstanding features in this lush, verdant area are the giant tree ferns, *Dicksonia antarctica*.

Architectural structures figure prominently in the original garden design. A classical summerhouse was positioned on a site from which the romantic views across the gardens and estate could be seen to best advantage. The Target House, where once the family practised archery, now houses a small garden exhibition, and the original game larder and the unusually ornamental privy are still intact and on the viewing itinerary. The garden has a further unique feature, a mischievous piece of deception in the shape of an 'eye catcher' or folly, the ruined façade of a building like a small stone cottage improbably sited at the top of a steep bank and now heavily cloaked in ivy.

Members of the Thellusson family continued to live on the estate until 1990. When English Heritage took over the property, both the house and gardens were in need of restoration, and an extensive and sensitive programme of work was begun before the house and gardens opened to the public in 1995. With the help of family paintings and photographs taken of the gardens throughout the 19th and early 20th centuries it has been possible to turn back the clock and restore them with almost complete authenticity.

So successfully has this been achieved, indeed, that it is scarcely possible for the visitor to distinguish between original and recent features. The gardens and parkland now merit Grade II* English Heritage status.

With the Italianate topiary now back in shape and forming the formal structure of so much of the gardens, more swathes and banks of colour have been added to ensure that the property has something new to offer month by month. In February and March there is the breathtaking sight of some 500,000 snowdrops and over 30 varieties of daffodil, many of them growing, naturally, in long grass. In April the floral tapestry changes as, in some years, at least 5,000 tulips take over, and in May and June both the Rose Garden and the wild flower meadows attract the most attention. Grassy areas around the property are neither close-cut nor treated with herbicides, so wild flowers including orchids, restharrow, milkwort and cowslips flourish in this natural environment, a remnant of magnesium limestone grassland. Just as they were in former times, the summer bedding plants are at their peak in beds, borders and urns in late June and July when the ferns, too, are seen at their best. The woodland walks, beautiful throughout the year, become more and more vibrant as autumn progresses, and then in winter the original garden design, structured as it is with myriad sculpture-like topiary shapes, becomes all-important.

The Brodsworth estate, situated on a limestone ridge that runs across South Yorkshire, was developed in the 18th century into a country gentleman's estate with an impressive mansion, in an area where there are known to have been medieval villages and a medieval nunnery. Now archaeologists have discovered that there are Iron Age and Roman enclosures and field systems and, on neighbouring property, the sites of several Neolithic long barrows. Extensive investigation using the latest equipment and techniques and including a geophysical survey is now being undertaken. It is hoped that it will establish the identity of the earliest inhabitants of this ridge where, a century and a half ago, Charles Thellusson demolished the Georgian mansion and built his new country home.

Among the old roses in the Rose Garden there is *Rosa mundi*, the Gallica rose which has splashes of pink and white on a crimson background and dates from the 12th century. It was said to have been named after Rosamund, the mistress of King Henry II, *R.* There are also 'Blush Noisette', a blush-pink shrub rose from the 18th century, one of the first Noisettes, *R.* 'Boule de Neige', a pure white rose dating from 1867, and *R.* 'Cécile Brünner' a delicate soft-pink China shrub rose from 1881.

Right: The Fern Dell reflects the Victorian passion for these plants, known as pteridomania

DALEMAIN Cumbria CA11 0HB

Just to the north of Ullswater, in the magnificent countryside of Cumbria, is Dalemain. The estate seems to have evolved over time in a most natural way, from 12th-century pele tower with its kitchen garden, to an Elizabethan knot garden furnished with herbs; a Stuart terrace dating from 1680 is still to be seen. In the 18th century the building was given a fine new façade, and apple trees such as 'Nonsuch' and 'Keswick

Codling' were planted, which still bear fruit today. The gardens have been skilfully re-established by the present owners, Mr and Mrs Robert Hasell-McCosh, so that a visit to Dalemain is pervaded by that sense of continuity which is so strong an element in good gardening.

The Terrace Walk, with its buttressed retaining wall, is much as it was when Sir Edward Hasell laid it out in the 17th

century, although there are now several rambling roses on the wall that attempt to invade the gravel path, and a deep herbaceous border below the walls of the house. At the end of the terrace is a handsome Grecian fir with the Knot Garden in its shadow. Rather reduced in size during the last century, the knot has a marble fountain as its central feature, and consists of low, symmetrical box hedges filled to overflowing with herbs, campanulas and antirrhinums, while the old Victorian Vine Border has the massed seasonal colour of shrub roses, spirea and lilies.

From the knot, the ground slopes upwards to the west with, on one side of a gravel path, a lawn planted with old apples, plums and pears. On the other side is a deep border with splendid shrub roses edged with sedums, phloxes, rodgersias, meconopsis and irises and, at the top of the garden, a classical summerhouse built into an alcove.

A door leads into Lob's Wood where a path winds between beech and oak trees on the top of a steep bank above the Dacre Beck. Further along the wall is a fine pavilion, with a pointed roof and mullioned windows, dating from 1550. A flight of steep steps leads down to the Wild Garden, started by Sylvia McCosh, the current owner's mother, which is bright with drifts of daffodils in spring, and with flowering trees and shrubs and the Himalayan blue poppy, *Meconopsis grandis*, in early summer.

The Children's Garden, a delightful feature developed by Mrs Hasell-McCosh when her children were young, features plants with 'animal' names, including bear's breeches (acanthus), snapdragon (antirrhinum) and foxglove (digitalis). More fun still, each plant is identified by locally hand-crafted wooden animal signs; similar examples are for sale in the estate's gift shop.

A visit to Dalemain is a particular pleasure, not only for the sense of historical continuity that it exudes, but for the wonderfully dense vegetation – the result of knowledgeable gardening and the climate of Lakeland.

GRESGARTH HALL Lancashire LA2 9NB

½ mile (0.8km) south of Kendal | **Open selected days Easter to Oct** | **Tel: 01524 771838** | **www.arabellalennoxboyd.com**

The gloriously productive Kitchen Garden at Gresgarth might be considered a microcosm of the garden design as a whole, made up as it is of separate beds – small squares and larger ones, rectangles, triangles and curves – each with its own ingredients, colour scheme and intricate patterns,all coming together like pieces of a horticultural jigsaw to make a complete picture.

The garden surrounding the honey-gold, castellated house is composed in a similar way of a variety of elements – colour-themed gardens, luxuriant herbaceous borders, a serpentine walk, bog and lakeside garden, wild garden, orchard and nuttery – that combine to display a versatility of moods and styles and yet compose an integrated design.

The Gresgarth Hall garden is the vision of Arabella Lennox-Boyd, a renowned garden designer, who moved here with her husband Sir Mark in 1978 when he became Member of Parliament for a Lancashire constituency. Italian-born and brought up in Rome, Lady Lennox-Boyd brought with her the Italian sense of formality and theatre, but she had already fallen in love with the English romantic style of soft, gentle colour drifts and understatement.

At Gresgarth she has achieved a delightful marriage of the two styles. The centre of the design, remarkable for its lack of detail, is a circular, closely mown lawn, its restraint seeming to accentuate the ambitious and varied planting radiating from it. In front of the house herbaceous borders protected by yew hedges are a watercolour palette in summer of blues, pinks and magentas with delphinium, campanula, lavender, old roses, pelargoniums and peonies tumbling together in a romantically pretty way. By autumn stronger hues are introduced with fiery dahlias and rudbeckias sharing the limelight with purple foliage plants.

Throughout the garden there is a marriage of classical and modern statuary. A cobble mosaic of an olive tree has unmistakable Italian overtones. Formal steps and terraces encroached by cascades of fragrant roses lead down from the house to a lake where, as in the Bog Garden, there is a cacophony of moisture-loving plants – of wildlife, too.

Trees are an important and dominant feature of the landscape and garden at Gresgarth. The house is at the head of a small valley with a river running through it and is surrounded on three sides by hills covered by majestic oaks and beech and comprising an arboretum where there is a collection of magnolias, styrax, halesia, stewartias, acers, sorbus and cornus. Ferns and hellebores flourish under the leaf cover of rhododendrons and other interesting shrubs. A moss-and-fern-covered *meta sudans*, a tall, narrow pyramid down which water trickles, contributes both height and formality and is at the centre of a thicket of *Betula utilis* species (Himalayan birch). A massed planting of white cherries throws a veil of blossom over the slope facing the house and is all the more striking for the underplanting of white daffodils.

Pleached limes separate a series of garden rooms from the surrounding parkland; these act as a wind break from the lethal westerly winds. Arabella Lennox-Boyd has always eschewed the kind of design that encloses a garden within restrictive boundary walls or fences, preferring to create the impression that the garden melts – fades – into its surroundings. Here at Gresgarth Hall, where the Artle Beck, a tributary of the Lune, defines one border and trees merge into the distant parkland beyond, it certainly does.

Arabella Lennox-Boyd has been awarded six Gold Medals for gardens she has designed at the RHS Chelsea Flower Show, one of which won the Best in Show award. Displaying the versatility that is evident in her garden at Gresgarth Hall, her entries ranged from a slate rill and a series of bubble fountains to commemorate the centenary of the National Trust, through a formal terrace and topiary garden, to a romantic ruin inspired by the Italian gardens at Ninfa.

Left: The Japanese *Acer seiryu* by the quirkily designed Kitchen Garden gate

Above: Blossom above the terraces in spring

189

HERTERTON HOUSE
Northumberland NE61 4BN

2 miles (3km) north of Cambo | Open selected days Easter to Oct | Tel: 01670 774278

Herterton House stands high in the uplands of Northumberland. When Frank and Marjorie Lawley came here in 1976 the Tudor house was nearly derelict, and the disused farmyard was littered with broken farm implements and waist high in stinging nettles. Today, with great gardening skill and far-sighted vision, all is restored and the gardens are not only delightful and wholly individual, but contain many unusual hardy plants which are also on sale in the adjoining nursery area.

Five separate gardens have been created at Herterton, the last being the Nursery Garden. The first, a small formal layout, fronts onto the road. An evergreen garden in green and gold, it has as its centrepiece a number of topiary features in clipped yew and several varieties of box. Beneath the house wall, which is draped with jasmines, honeysuckles and a fragrant form of *Clematis montana* 'Wilsonii', box-edged beds contain lilies, crown imperials and dicentras.

A gravel path bordered with cream and white fumitory leads into what is now a physic garden laid out as a knot. This charming garden has geometric beds of medicinal herbs including tansy, camphor and hyssop edged with *Saxifraga x urbium*

'Elliott's Variety', while a weeping pear stands in the centre. Roses in this enclosure, together with the honeysuckle that covers the surrounding walls, give off a heady fragrance in summer.

Behind the house is the largest of the enclosures, a walled flower garden. Regular beds separated by gravel paths have been planted in accordance with an overall colour scheme. Here there is a profusion of old-

Above: The vibrant companion planting of *Allium sphaerocephalon* and *Achillea* 'Terracotta'

fashioned daisies, with pinks, wallflowers, campions and buttercups, while campanulas, violas, geraniums, avens (geum) and Jacob's ladder give the impression of a cottage garden deep in the countryside but, surely, in a more southerly climate.

The fourth enclosure is a parterre of miniature box nostalgically called the Fancy Garden because such designs were often taken from embroideries, known as 'fancy work'. Beyond this, on a low terrace, there is a gazebo where Marjorie Lawley's planting plans of the garden are displayed. From an upper room there are wide and contrasting views of the landscape to the north, and the house and a panorama of the gardens – evidence of the planting plans come to fruition – to the south.

It says much for the planning and horticultural skills of the Lawleys that a garden of such romance and beauty can be created 700 feet (212 metres) above sea level in such a seemingly unlikely, windswept environment.

Below: Perfect symmetry in the flower garden

LEVENS HALL Cumbria LA8 0PD

5 miles (8km) south of Kendal | Open selected days Easter to mid-Oct | Tel: 01539 560321 | www.levenshall.co.uk

What do 'Queen Elizabeth and her Maids of Honour', 'The Judge's Wig', 'The Bellingham Lion' and 'The Jugs of 'Morocco' have in common? They are the affectionate and fanciful names given to some of the 90 topiary structures that adorn and dominate the gardens at Levens Hall. These living sculptures, some of the oldest in the world, have survived true to the original designs for over 300 years and make the gardens a place of horticultural pilgrimage for a great many garden-lovers.

The property originally consisted of only a square, fortified (pele) tower built on the lower reaches of the River Kent in 1350 by the de Redman family as a defence against the threat of Scottish raiders from over the border. In the mid-16th century their descendants, the Bellingham family, built an Elizabethan house around the tower and in 1688 it passed into the hands of Colonel James Grahme, a cousin of Alan Bellingham, who added the east and south wings. It passed from Colonel Grahme to his daughter Catherine who became Countess of Suffolk, and later to the Bagot family.

The history of the Levens Hall garden begins with Colonel Grahme's ownership. A Jacobean nobleman who held the office of Keeper of the Privy Purse to King James II, he brought with him a young French gardener, Guillaume Beaumont, who had been a pupil of André Le Nôtre in the gardens of the Palace of Versailles, Paris. Beaumont, who had recently finished laying out the Hampton Court Palace gardens, spent the last 40 years of his life working at Levens Hall. A portrait of him that hangs in the Hall has the inscription: 'Gardener to King James II and Colonel James Grahme'.

Beaumont began work on the gardens in 1694 and 300 years later, to celebrate the partnership of Colonel Grahme and his gardener and their enduring inspiration, a fountain garden bordered by pleached limes was created.

The fashion for gardens featuring precisely clipped evergreens began in Holland, travelled through France and arrived in England in the late 17th century, coinciding with Colonel Grahme's arrival at Levens Hall. Beaumont's imagination knew no limits and he created designs, some now over 20 feet (6 metres) high, representing graceful birds, elegant beasts, chess pieces – some quaintly reminiscent of episodes from Lewis Carroll's *Alice's Adventures in Wonderland* – cones, spirals, pyramids, giant rings, arches and even teacups and saucers.

Over the years successive gardeners, charged with maintaining these sculptural masterpieces, have added tails to birds, curlicues to wigs, handles to teacups and other refinements without altering the spirit of the original designs.

Beaumont's design for the garden consisted of more than the yew and box sculptures. He created a series of garden walks and planted extensive beech hedging that in summer is seen as a 16-foot (5-metre) high crisp green wall and in winter displays its superstructure of massive, gnarled and twisted trunks: a sculpture of a different kind. This innovative gardener is also credited with

Left: **The topiary structures at Levens Hall are some of the oldest in the world**

Above: **A lead planter in the garden dated 1704**

creating the first known example of a ha-ha, a sunken ditch designed to keep cattle out of the gardens without a fence interrupting the view.

Visitors to the garden are always incredulous at the formidable amount of maintenance needed to keep the topiary masterpieces in shape. Work begins in August when a team of five gardeners starts trimming the beech hedge. Then in October, when the garden is closed to visitors, they start clipping the massive topiary structures. The evergreen sculptures are clad in scaffolding and trimmed with petrol clippers, an arduous task that can last well into the following year.

These ancient sculptures are so firmly established that they are able to recover from seasonal damage. Heavy snow can play havoc with the intricate shapes so that they take a while to regain their crisp outlines. Two of the sculptures took a year to recover from damage caused when a tree felled by a storm crashed on top of them. Some of the oldest structures now lean drunkenly in ways

that were not intended; but perhaps that only adds to their charm.

The topiary structures and a parterre with beds edged with low box hedges – more work for the shearers – are planted twice a year with some 15,000 seasonal bedding plants, a glorious sight in both early summer and autumn. In spring large carpets of naturalised snakeskin lilies (*Fritillaria meleagris*) punctuated by thick ribbons of cream narcissus enliven the ground down to the river.

When visitors have marvelled enough at the topiary eccentricities, the garden has yet more to offer. There is a small orchard, a nuttery and a herb garden. The Rose Garden is a delight in summer and the long herbaceous borders are planted to maintain colour and interest over many months. An undulating avenue of oaks leads to the parkland where a herd of black fallow deer and the famous Bagot goats – a rare breed with long, curved horns – roam. Levens Park was also laid out by Guillaume Beaumont.

'The Jugs of Morocco' name given to one of the topiary sculptures refers to a dark, spiced ale brewed from a secret family recipe dating from Elizabethan times. It was named Morocco Ale by Colonel Grahme, who associated it with the dark beers of Tangiers. The ale was matured for 21 years and served in the Levens Hall garden in May every year at the annual Radish Feast. Guests were required to stand on one leg while drinking the brew and pledge 'Luck to Levens while t'Kent flows'.

Not surprisingly Levens Hall, a property that dates back over so many centuries, has attracted a number of ghost stories. It is said that a Grey Lady appears in front of cars on the driveway; that a friendly woman wearing a print dress and cap appears only to visiting children, and that a small black dog wanders the Hall.

NEWBY HALL
North Yorkshire HG4 5AE

4 miles (6.5km) south east of Ripon | Open selected days Apr to late Sep | Tel: 0845 450 4068 | www.newbyhall.com

Newby Hall is set in immaculate parkland on the banks of the River Ure. Built at the end of the 17th century in the manner of Sir Christopher Wren and altered by Robert Adam a century later, Newby is one of the great houses of Yorkshire – a county rich in architectural gems – and its gardens are equally notable. They were created by Major Edward Compton in the 1920s and 1930s; later, during the time of Mr Robin Compton, the double herbaceous border took on its unique planting style.

The plan of the garden is based on two main axes. One, the Statue Walk, which has Venetian figures backed by a hedge of *Prunus cerasifera* 'Pissardii', lies along the south front of the house. The other, north/south axis runs at right angles from the Lily Pond. It holds the house majestically at the top of the double border and slopes down to the River Ure below. Backed by a great yew hedge, the towering spires of delphiniums in late June are a glorious sight, their colours shading from white through palest pinks and blues to lavender and deep purple. Red and pink roses are there, too, with campanulas, eryngiums and great clumps of *Cephalaria gigantea* (giant scabious) with their pin-

cushion-like heads of yellow flowers. Later, during August and September, dahlias feature, their vibrancy backed up by annuals including the spidery-flowered cleome, nicotiana, *Salvia horminum* and the magenta-pink-flowering *S.microphylla* 'Cerro Potosi'.

The popular Rhododendron Walk is densely planted with magnolias and camellias, while the sunken Rose Garden is enclosed by a copper beech hedge, balanced on the other side of the central borders by the Autumn Garden.

The Autumn Garden is a compartmental walled garden on the site of the old croquet

lawn. The wall was erected in the mid-1990s to give protection to the more tender shrubs such as the sweet-smelling *Clerodendron trichotomum* var. *fargesii* with the intriguing common name, Farges harlequin glory bower. Here there are late-summer-flowering herbaceous plants with salvias in a wide range of heights and colours again playing a significant role. They include *Salvia microphylla* 'Newby Hall' with its blood-red flowers, the distinct *S. discolor* with its silvery-grey foliage and almost black flowers, and the pure blue *S. patens* that can be grown from seed.

Dahlias are specially selected to give an exuberant and colourful display of varying heights and flower forms with exotic purples,

radiant reds, blousy pinks, moody maroons and many more forming the backbone of the planting. This is done on an annual basis with some 600 plants all grown in-house. As a consequence the Autumn Garden varies from year to year.

Close to the Lily Pond is Sylvia's Garden, named after Mr Compton's grandmother. Surrounded by a dark yew hedge (which is currently being restored) the garden is planted on formal lines although the overall effect is soft and subtle. The colour palette is tranquil, achieved mainly with a wonderful collection of foliage plants complementing whites, pinks, purples and blues enlivened with touches of soft yellow and magenta. A quiet and peaceful haven, this garden encourages the visitor to linger and reflect a while.

The Rose Pergola, covered with climbers and ramblers and underplanted with a variety of hostas, leads down to a fascinating rock

garden, incorporating a waterfall and many damp-loving plants, designed in about 1900 by the great gardener Ellen Willmott, who owned the Warley Place estate in Essex and was awarded the Victoria Medal of Honour by the Royal Horticultural Society.

With the national collection of cornus (dogwood) trees in flower from mid-May to early July; a striking Lime Avenue and even a Tropical Garden with rodgersias, yuccas, eryngiums, phormiums, rheums and magnolias, Newby Hall is one of the most notable gardens in the north of England. As part of an ongoing programme of improvements, the herbaceous border will be overhauled, starting at the top end. Replanting will continue over the next three years, finishing the last beds in 2015. The changes will be very gradual, but the drawing up of a full plan, and the introduction of new specimens will result in a slow-dawning transformation.

Left: A place for tranquil contemplation, Sylvia's Garden is enclosed by a dark yew hedge

Above: Newby Hall's elegant South Front, seen from the herbaceous border

An avenue of limes curtaining a vivacious spring-flowering border; a wild flower meadow that displays naturalistic planting at its very best; a grove of trees with leaves that turn from bronze through yellow to purple; a silent garden of evergreen columns around a reflective pool – all these elements and more have been created within the walls of the former kitchen garden that once kept the household at Scampston Hall self-sufficient in fruit, vegetables and herbs, and, more recently, where Christmas trees were grown for sale.

Sir Charles and Lady Legard, who came to the property in 1987, first turned their attention to the 17th-century house and the surrounding Capability Brown-modelled parkland. Then in 1998 they called in Dutch designer Piet Oudolf to remodel the kitchen garden and create an excitingly modern design within its walls. When the dilapidated glasshouses and gardeners' quarters were demolished, leaving only the listed greenhouse, the fig house and a pool, Oudolf had an almost blank canvas on which to sketch a patchwork of garden rooms with widely varying characteristics, yet with a feeling of oneness.

The result is thrilling. Entrance to the garden leads immediately into the Plantsman's Walk which runs along three sides of the original wall and is marked by an avenue of 200 limes. In the 10-foot (3-metre) perimeter bed, spring-flowering shrubs, all underplanted with bulbs, include tree peonies, *Paeonia rockii*, their large, waxy white-petalled flowers blotched with maroon, and *Edgeworthia chrysantha*, noted for its rounded heads of fragrant yellow flowers in winter and early spring. In autumn, colour in the borders is achieved with flowering hydrangea and the rice-paper plant, *Tetrapanax papyrifer*, whose bold sprays of creamy-yellow summer and autumn flowers are replaced by black berries in winter.

A naturalistic perennial meadow in front of the conservatory is a keynote feature of Piet Oudolf's work. Planted around a circular dipping pond, it is spattered with flower colour from the end of May until late autumn. First there is a kaleidoscopic pattern of red and yellow, purple and orange. Shake the kaleidoscope a little, and later in the year the colour pattern is dominated by green and brown, yellow and black foliage, seedheads and grasses which by then can be appreciated almost individually for their shape and form.

Planted as a backdrop to the perennial meadow, the Katsura Grove is a woodland in miniature, dramatically highlighted by the inclusion of the *Cercidiphyllum japonicum* whose leaves from spring to autumn turn through almost all the colours of the rainbow. Yew hedges, sober by comparison, are not yet fully formed. When they are they will have straight edges and sides but serpentine tops, the undulations lending an air of informality to this dense evergreen shrub.

Clipped and shaped yew and box feature prominently throughout the Walled Garden, used in many different ways to convey a variety of ideas. In the Spring and Summer Box Gardens, each of which has a seasonal herbaceous border, widely spaced 3-foot (1-metre) cubes of box are to have, respectively, domed and dished tops. In the Silent Garden, rows of clipped yew columns, each one standing on a square, clipped base, are doubly effective as they are reflected in the clear water of the square pool.

And in the Serpentine Garden, six rows of clipped yew hedges, all with undulating tops, encourage visitors to weave between the lines and discover the concealed herbaceous beds beyond.

There are no formal lawns in this excitingly unorthodox walled garden but – an infinitely more original feature – an area that the owners call 'drifts of grass'. Divided by a path and inset with bench seats, patches of mown grass are alternated with thick, curving swathes of tufty molinia grass, attractive for its light-as-a-feather movement in the slightest breeze, and for the long purple spikelets it produces in late summer.

Climb a flight of steps to the top of the Mount, a decapitated grassed pyramid in the centre of the garden, and it all becomes clear – how the pieces of the patchwork fit together; how this former kitchen garden has been transformed with ingenuity and flair, within a park laid out by Capability Brown.

Brown's scheme for the 80-acre (32ha) parkland had so pleased Sir William St Quintin, the then owner of Scampston Hall and an ancestor of the present owner, that in a letter to Brown he wrote that the design 'answers prodigiously well' to his requirements. Visitors to the remodelled walled garden would surely echo those sentiments today, with reference to Piet Oudolf's design.

One of the most delightful elements of the Walled Garden at Scampston Hall is the 'drifts of grass' area with its curving swathes of molinia grass planted amongst the mown areas. The grass is not difficult to grow and propagates prodigiously – the 6,000 plants now forming the swathes began as a planting of only 50.

Some of the molinia grasses grow to great heights – *M. altissima* can reach 8 feet (2.5m). The variegated form, known as variegated purple moor grass, which has yellow and green striped leaves and, in late summer, purple spikelets, grows to 2 feet (60cm). The grasses prefer acid soil and need a dry, sunny position.

Many other grasses and sedges would create a similar effect when planted in mown grass in strips, swathes or clumps. Bowles' golden sedge, *Carex elata* 'Aurea', which has golden-yellow leaves and blackish-brown flower spikes in autumn, reaches a height of 16 inches (40cm). For a more feather-like effect, you could try planting squirrel tail grass, *Hordeum jubatum,* which can grow to 24 inches (60cm) and has arches of silky, creamy-golden plumes.

YEWBARROW HOUSE

High above sea level and with glorious coastal views, this garden, so at home in its northern landscape, has exciting areas of exotic planting and is growing in interest year by year.

The sand and sea merging with the far horizon over Morecambe Bay seem to compose a blank canvas against which Jonathan Denby has painted his vibrant and ever-changing garden. The use of local slate and limestone to create snaking paths, dividing walls and structural features gives the 4½-acre (1.8ha) garden of Yewbarrow House a fitting sense of place, a carefully planned space entirely at one with its surroundings.

In only 11 years the area which previously saw its heyday in Victorian times has been transformed from a near-wilderness of brambles, unkempt trees and shrubs to a garden and woodland with purpose. The purpose – the owner's vision – was to create a coastal haven with year-round colour, a variety of moods and, to the delight of visitors, a number of surprises.

On an exposed, sloping site on England's north-west coast one might not expect to see exotic plants native to far warmer climes. And yet here at Yewbarrow House, where frost rarely penetrates the ground, there are olive trees that bear fruitful if modest crops; mimosa that sparkles like sunlight against the neutral background of a ruined stone bridge; and myriad exciting plants that are native to Mexico, Hawaii, Africa, Australia and New Zealand.

Just as local materials have been used to construct paths and architectural features that look as if they might have played host to

Left: Containerised phormiums provide 'weight' and structure against dense planting

Right: In its glorious coastal setting, the hot spring doubles as a heated swimming pool

naturalised plants for centuries, so evergreen plants have been amassed to create a verdant background that, attractive in its own right, serves to highlight the colour and form of both modest and showy flowers.

Gradient is a significant factor. The garden at the front of the house which has the steepest of slopes, around 45 degrees, has been planted with hundreds of large evergreens to minimise maintenance and create a looking-down-on-the-clouds effect. Only the formal lawn in the Sunken Garden is on the level. This grassy patch, defined by slate paths and high banks, has a striking central feature: a tall, straight-as-can-be *Cordyline australis*, known as New Zealand

cabbage palm, its frondy umbrella far too elevated to offer shade. At one end of the lawn, a curved stone seat supported by three lion figures is veiled throughout the summer with white daisy-like marguerites, a triumph of contrasting textures. Like a balcony overlooking the stage, a high bank of *Hebe parviflora angustifolia*, with its cloud-like clusters of snow-white flowers and decorative evergreen foliage, forms a thick hummock the year round, while on the other side is a curtain of cardoons and dense evergreens.

Move into the Italian Terrace and the mood of the garden changes from restrained to exuberant and the planting might change

from year to year. Where once there was dense planting of cannas there might now be dahlias, displayed to superb effect in alternating rows of burnt-orange and lemon-yellow flowers. Dahlias have become a speciality at Yewbarrow House; shows and competitions are held there, space is given to a trial ground, and the head gardener prides himself on his success with saving and growing the seed. Juxtaposed with familiar garden plants there are notable rarities such as uhdeas, native Mexican plants known as tree daisies which were popular in Victorian times but have been little known for decades; the so-called false banana, *Ensete maurelii*, an African native whose burgundy-washed-with-green leaves form a distinctive vase shape; and the succulent *Aeonium* 'Schwarzkopf' which has rosettes of narrow purple leaves and, it is hoped, will eventually be crowned in spring by pyramids of golden flowers.

The Japanese Garden, perhaps the most surprising feature in this Cumbrian environment, was created around a hot spring that doubles as a heated swimming pool. The boiler and filter are concealed in the ornamental teahouse; stone pagoda-like ornaments reinforce the Oriental theme and the area is enlivened by a deep bank of yellow and orange azaleas.

Ferns self-seed wherever the spores are carried in the garden and are allowed to grow there only until they are ready to be transplanted to the Fern Garden, where they provide dense ground cover beneath the feature plants. These include several species of tree ferns (all of which need to be watered freely in a dry summer) such as the frost-tender cyatheas, the palm-like *Dicksonia squarrosa*, and *D. antarctica*, known as the Australian tree fern, which can reach a height of 20 feet (6 metres).

Height is a feature in the Gravel Garden, too. An exercise in restraint, this area is formalised with rows of circular beds mulched with gravel and edged with stones. Most display a single plant to full advantage. Here, the Mexican beschorneria, a clump-forming succulent with greyish-green, sword-shaped leaves up to 3 feet (1 metre) long and, in spring, spikes of tubular flowers twice that length; there, specimens of *Echium pininana*, known as tree echium or the pride of Tenerife, which were planted as seeds and, in only three years, attained a height of 14 feet (4 metres). This is a plant that enjoys a maritime situation, attracts bees and hoverflies and in summer is covered with thousands of small blue bell-shaped flowers.

Above: The terraces rise steeply on this sloping site

Right: Dahlias are a speciality here, with many raised from seed

Amongst these almost other-worldly plants there is a gazebo and, seated on a stone wall, a life-size bronze of Jonathan and Margaret Denby's eldest daughter, Joanna.

Any area of the garden that has not already been planned and skilfully planted is constantly under review: its turn will come. Thus the long drive that bisects the garden has now become the Olive Grove, enriched and enlivened by gloriously twisted and twirled ancient olive trees interplanted with gnarled old vines. These magnificent specimens form an avenue leading to the Meathop Bridge Arch which was constructed from stone recycled from a redundant humpback bridge.

In this northernmost part of the garden, backing onto Yewbarrow Wood, there was once a polytunnel; it is no more. Its place has been taken by The Orangery, housing mammoth colocasias, ensettes and strelitzias which, appreciating these most favourable conditions, tripled in size within a year. The terrace outside The Orangery is a mosaic by Maggy Howarth which was originally a focal point in Jonathan Denby's Beekeeper's Garden at the Hampton Court Flower Show. The aviary from that garden has now been reconstructed behind the Meathop Bridge Arch.

Whereas so much of the Yewbarrow House garden is decorative, restful, inspirational, the Victorian Kitchen Garden also has work to do – to provide fruit, vegetables and herbs not just 'for the house', as in days gone by, but for the owner's three neighbouring hotels. It is entirely organic – no chemicals at all are used – and worked on the crop rotation system. Some plots are laid out on the knot-garden principle with saladings and herbs planted in distinctive patterns, colour contrasted with colour within each geometric area; others are in soldierly rows. Visitors, please note a construction not to be missed. The potting shed, the powerhouse of the vegetable garden, was recently built around two beautiful Pre-Raphaelite stained-glass windows.

At the top of the Yewbarrow House site there is a large cutting garden with row upon row of flowers that, like the produce, will be sent to the hotels. From one season to the next, this area is perhaps the most painterly of all, a palette of colour etched against the sometimes grey, sometimes blue vista of Morecambe Bay.

A small patio or gravel garden can be given the 'Yewbarrow House look' with one or more Mexican beschorneria plants which, being almost stemless, form a fan shape close to the ground. The plants are half hardy, need full sun and well-drained soil. Propagate by dividing the leaf rosettes at the base in spring or summer.

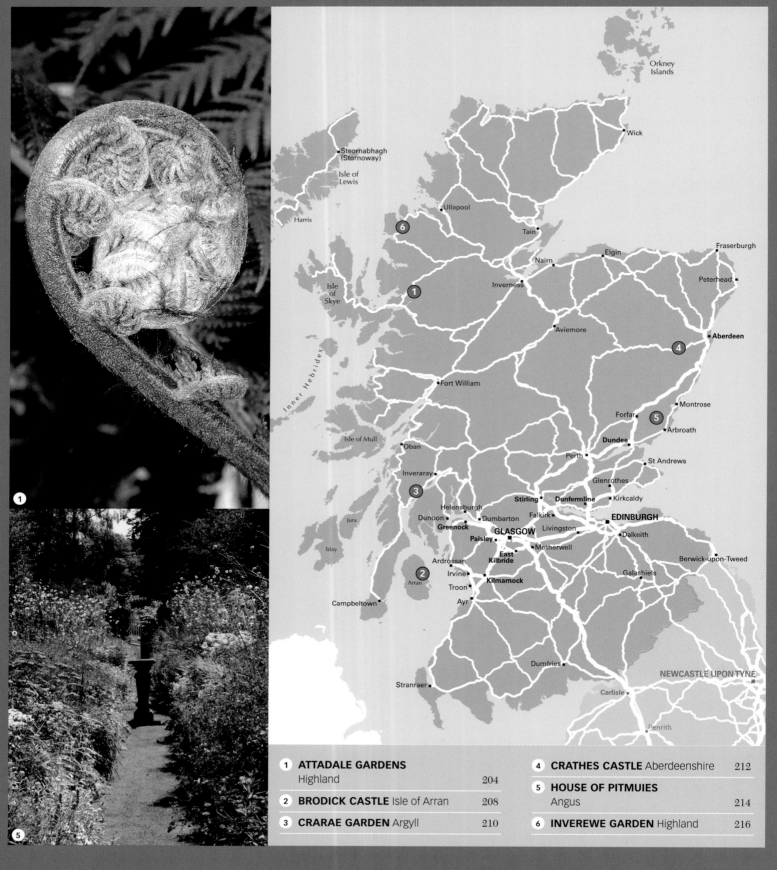

SCOTLAND & THE BORDERS | 6

Gardens in this region offer the visitor walks – often long walks – on the wild side, with breathtaking views, variously, of lochs and burns, mountains and glens. Magnificent rhododendrons are showcased in a garden with latitude more northerly than that of Moscow; elsewhere there is a water garden planted with almost sub-tropical profusion and described as a Monet-like dream; a raked gravel garden with a strong Japanese influence; walled gardens burgeoning with herbs and cottage-garden plants; and, yes, there are castles too.

One can walk for miles through this magnificent north-west Scotland coastal scenery and never leave the Attadale estate, which stretches from the south shore of Loch Carron inland to Loch Monar, 15 miles (24km) to the east. The house was built in 1755 in a well-chosen spot sheltered by the hill from the prevailing north-west wind. The 20-acre (8ha) garden has gradually evolved around it.

The estate was historically part of the Clan Matheson lands and it was a member of that family, Sir Alexander Matheson, who was responsible for building the railway from Inverness to Strome. In the 1880s Attadale was leased and subsequently in 1910 bought by Baron Schroder of the German banking family. His son, Captain William Schroder, laid out the garden creating hill paths for his

trees and rhododendrons and an elaborate rose garden with pergolas, topiary birds and numerous small beds.

When Ian Macpherson bought the estate in 1952 the trees had taken over the garden – even the rhododendrons struggled in their shade. The flower beds were overgrown with grass and bracken; the woodland criss-crossed with rabbit wire.

Left: Tender ferns in the geodesic dome

Above: Intriguing detail of *Dicksonia antarctica*

Right: The old mill stream in near-sub-tropical profusion

Devastating storms ravaged the garden in 1984 and again in 1989, changing the face of the garden forever. Thousands of trees were destroyed. At the same time, old paths and steps that had been hidden for years were revealed. Ewen and Nicky Macpherson who had inherited the estate in 1984 seized the opportunity to remodel the garden on lines that reflected their own interests.

The old mill stream beside the drive had been widened into a series of ponds and small waterfalls linked by elegant bridges; the banks behind them planted in almost sub-tropical profusion with gunnera and other large-leaved plants contrasted with bamboos and grasses. Glorious blue mecanopsis and the brilliant colours of the Himalayan primulas are reflected in the dark, peaty water between the waterlilies. The area has been described as a Monet dream!

New steps and paths lead to the old Rhododendron Walk. *Viburnum mariesii,* eucryphia, white azaleas and crinodendron have been added to the old rhododendrons, backed by unusual conifers such as *Abies koreana* with its violet-blue cones and the Bhutan pine with its slender silver needles. At the end of the walk, a viewing platform has been built with splendid views of the house and down Loch Carron to the Cuillins of Skye. Below it, against the cliff, is another closely planted border of astilbe, primula, meconopsis and darmera, whose plate-like leaves turn scarlet in autumn.

The Macphersons' sculpture collection can be seen throughout the garden. A bronze heron by Elizabeth MacDonald Buchanan

is reflected in the pond; an eagle by Rosie Sturgis stands on a rocky outcrop by the viewpoint; the abstract shapes of bronze birds by Bridget McCrum perch on a rock by the waterfall and on an old stone roller below the Rhododendron Walk. Another bronze, a chameleon by Alex Jones, climbs on an old rhododendron in the Fern Garden, and the outstanding life-sized cheetah by Hamish Mackie turns on a rock below the viewpoint, a marvel of balanced movement.

To enliven a dark ring of rhododendrons to the west of the house, Nicky Macpherson designed a giant sundial. The gnomon is supported by a modern rendering of the Macpherson rampant cat carved by Graciela Ainsworth of Edinburgh.

The Sunken Garden, surrounded by dry-stone walls and *Rosa rugosa* hedges, planned to give colour all through the year, has been planted to resemble a Persian carpet, each quadrant repeating in reverse the pattern of its neighbour. Only low-growing plants are used in this windswept area of the garden, the colours chosen to echo not contrast with the landscape.

An avenue of Japanese birch (*Betula ermanii*) leads to a gateway into the Japanese Garden where lichened rocks and raked

Above: Orderly rows of beds in the Kitchen Garden

Right: From a viewing platform there are distant views of the Cuillins of Skye

gravel imitate the Mystic Islands of the West and the River of Life. A shakkei (or borrowed landscape) reveals the Applecross Hills, substituting for Mount Fuji. Reclaimed in 2002 from a flooded basin infested with weeds, this is now a quiet area designed for peaceful contemplation.

Old quarries behind the house provide ideal shady, damp conditions for the Old Rhododendron Dell planted in 1911 and the Fern Garden started in 2001. Tender ferns are housed in a geodesic dome made of triangular panels and closely resembling in miniature one of the Eden Project domes. Below it, a sunken fern garden has been created revealing the recently uncovered

early 19th-century drain. It is surrounded by a phalanx of *Dicksonia antarctica*, some remarkable trillium and various hostas, whose broad leaves contrast well with the delicate filigree of the ferns.

After the controlled chaos of the woodland, the tour of the Attadale gardens finishes on an orderly note. A tribute to the head gardener Geoff Stephenson and his team, the Kitchen Garden is a neatness-freak's delight, with its immaculately kept and manicured raised beds, box and yew hedges and paved herb garden.

Plants are propagated in the greenhouses and tunnel for the garden and there are usually some for sale.

The conservatory no longer has white slatted benches supporting ranks of geraniums and fuchsias, as it did until recently. Now it has curved drystone walls supporting a mini landscape of sub-tropical plants and ferns and a tiny watercourse. It houses species that would not survive cold northern winters – datura and abutilon from the southern states of the USA, and aloes and crassula from South Africa.

In the backyard there is an eccentric 'do-it-yourself' tearoom called the Old Larder, with garden books to read and photographs of the development of the garden and cameos of its personnel. Maps show the origin of many of the plants.

BRODICK CASTLE
Isle of Arran KA27 8HY

3 miles (5km) south of Corrie | Open Apr to end Oct | Tel: 01770 302202 | **www.nts.org.uk**

Brodick Castle, with its magnificent gardens and designed landscape, rises majestically above Brodick Bay on the Isle of Arran. It was once owned and created by the Dukes of Hamilton, one of Scotland's grandest aristocratic families. Surrounding the castle are 178 acres (72ha) of gardens and historic designed landscape of outstanding scenic and aesthetic quality, within which can be seen an excellent horticultural collection.

Brodick has become a key west-coast garden as a result of the favourable growing conditions created by the influence of the Gulf Stream; the good soils; the high rainfall due to the property's proximity to the Goatfell mountain range; and also the shelter of canopy trees and the salt- and wind-resistant shrub layer – of exceptional importance to the emergence and survival of the garden.

In the mid-19th century the 11th Duke of Hamilton, his wife, Princess Marie of Baden, and W A Nesfield, an important figure in 19th-century landscape design,

introductions from plant collectors and gifts from Tresco.

In the later 20th century the National Trust for Scotland has maintained and enhanced the reputation and significance of the garden by continuing to introduce plants from seed-collecting expeditions, from other gardens and by propagation. The garden holds three designated National Collections of rhododendron sub-groups; furthermore, a reserve collection of plants from the notable Horlick Collection at Achamore Gardens in Gigha – one of the most southerly of the Hebridean islands – has been created and is maintained here.

Today, visitors can enjoy a spring stroll through the woodland beneath the massive and colourful spring blooms of *Rhododendron sinograde*, *R. protistum* and *R. magnificum* and enjoy the sweet scents of the *rhododendron* sub-group Maddenia collection. In summer and early autumn the beds and borders of the Upper Walled Garden – which dates from 1710 – are full of half-hardy plants and specialities such as *Cardiocrinum giganteum* (giant lily) and *Cordyline banksii* – flourishing because of the shelter provided by the massive sandstone walls.

Look for an intriguing feature in the surrounding walls, where there are examples of bee boles, also known as bee garths. These rows of wall niches were created to house bee skeps (hives) to encourage bees to produce honey close to the house and pollinate flowers and fruit crops.

brought a romantic quality to the wooded landscape, creating walks and ornamental garden pavilions – including the Bavarian Summerhouse – as well as planting specimen trees and rerouting the entrance drive. The 20th century saw the creation of the Woodland Garden and plant collection by the Duchess of Montrose, enriched by new

Left: The Walled Garden overlooking the Firth of Clyde, with the Ardrossan ferry in the distance

Top right: The Bavarian Summerhouse

Right: Gentle curves in the Pergola Walk

CRARAE GARDEN Argyll PA32 8YA

On the road that runs along the edge of Loch Fyne, north from Minard Castle towards Inveraray, is the wonderful glen garden of Crarae. Originally started by Grace, Lady Campbell in the early years of the 20th century, Crarae was inspired in part by her great nephew, Reginald Farrer – the plant collector and traveller who introduced into Britain a number of rhododendron species from his trips to Kansu in 1914 and to Upper Burma in 1919 – and perhaps also by Sir John Stirling-Maxwell of Pollok. Her son, Sir George Campbell, spent many years extending the original planting, eventually creating this 'Himalayan ravine' garden in a Highland glen. Sir George's son, Sir Ilay, continued to care for Crarae until the National Trust for Scotland acquired and reopened the garden to the public in 2002.

Above Crarae is Beinn Ghlas, and where the highest larches end you can see the type of natural scrub of oak, alder, hazel, birch and rowan that had to be cleared from the lower slopes when the garden was originally created. Beyond the lawns and the two large borders immediately around the lodge, there are fabulous views over Loch Fyne with, in spring, massed colour of azaleas and a splendid *Acer tschonoskii*. In spring, too, there are bluebell trails through many of the woodland areas.

Following the Crarae Burn further into the Upper Glen, the dramatic colours of rhododendrons and azaleas, set against a backdrop of decorative hardwoods, catch the eye. The shrub planting includes olearias and the New Zealand pittosporum, which grows strongly here.

Left: Vibrant colour contrast of blue Himalayan poppies (meconopsis) and red candle primula

Right: Steep slopes, rushing water and dense planting give the look of a Himalayan valley

Close to the waterfall viewpoint there is a fine Japanese dogwood, *Cornus kousa*, which turns in October to contrast dramatically with the red-leaved azaleas, witch hazel and *Disanthus cercidifolius*. When you reach the top bridge, azaleas give colour to the foreground and *Rhododendron davidsonianum* stands beyond, its tulle-like flowers ranging from pale pink to lilac-mauve. Among the hybrid rhododendrons at Crarae are 'Loderi King George', 'Dairymaid', 'Laura Aberconway' and 'Beauty of Littleworth'.

Autumn colour is further enhanced with sorbus, acers, liriodendrons, cotoneasters and berberis competing for attention. With the backdrop of waterfalls and the rushing Crarae Burn, this is indeed a garden of great beauty and individuality.

CRATHES CASTLE Aberdeenshire AB31 5QJ

The first view of Crathes Castle promises that it is just as a Scottish castle should be. The magnificent woodland of Royal Deeside opens up to reveal the romantic tower-house with its turret stairs set in flowing lawns and with eight 'garden rooms' full of colour, contrasting with dark-green topiary. It was not until Sir James Burnett and his wife, Sybil, came to Crathes in 1926 that the garden took on its present structure; the brilliance of its design and planting is their achievement. Today, the castle and gardens are under the care of the National Trust for Scotland.

On entering the gardens you come directly into the White Borders. Beyond the West Border, with its herbaceous plants of blue and pink, steps lead to the Aviary Border, which shows olearias, clematis, *Carpenteria californica* and a splendid *Magnolia wilsonii*. To the right is the Golden Garden, with *Viburnum opulus* 'Xanthocarpum', golden berberis, philadelphus, weigela and the rose 'Agnes'. Half-way down the White Borders there is a Portugal laurel, *Prunus lusitanica*; from this point the main herbaceous borders run up

to the glasshouses. Here, there are syringas, viburnums and an interesting *Dipteronia sinensis*, while the June Borders, with the dovecote as a focal point, are planted in the cottage-garden style, with lupins, bearded irises, pyrethrum and several varieties of Oriental poppies.

The Wild Garden is at its best during the autumn with photinias, osmanthus and *Philadelphus wilsonii* contrasting with sorbus and *Liriodendron tulipifera*. In the Upper Pool Garden, Lady Burnett took as her palette the colours yellow, red and bronze, and by

Left: An immaculate topiary hedge separates a formal lawn from a potpourri of colourful shrubs

Above: Restrained use of colour enhances the cool, clear water effect

Right: A garden room in the Walled Garden

combining unlikely plants – for example, old roses with heathers and the yellow *Coreopsis vecticillata* with the bronze-leaved form of the wild bugle – she achieved some remarkable effects. The Rose Garden is formally arranged with four triangular beds holding floribunda roses supported by viburnums, a group of crab apples and a pocket handkerchief tree. Clearly inspired both by Gertrude Jekyll and Lawrence Johnston at Hidcote, the gardens at Crathes Castle hold many treasures for the plant-lover and the garden visitor alike.

HOUSE OF PITMUIES

Angus DD8 2SN

1 mile (1.5km) south of Guthrie | Open daily Apr to Oct | Tel: 01241 828245 | **www.pitmuies.com**

The road east from Forfar follows the valley of the Lunan Water. Near to Guthrie is the House of Pitmuies, one of the loveliest estates in this part of Scotland, already rich in such properties. The harled three-storeyed mansion was rebuilt in 1730 by Mr Ogilvy, and records show that the Walled Garden was in existence 50 years later. The foundations of the modern garden are most probably Victorian, but the beauty and immaculate condition of the layout today are due to the late Mr Farquhar Ogilvie and his wife, Margaret.

Entering the gardens from the car park, you come first to the Kitchen Garden which, in traditional fashion, still provides vegetables, fruit and flowers for the house. Beyond, an archway of weeping pears introduces the central walk of the Summer Borders, flanked by hedges of red cherries and beds planted with soft-coloured summer flowers. Below the house, and linked by stone steps, are three gardens of great beauty and variety. Around a central fountain, with tall bulrushes and waterlilies, ferns, alpines and mallows grow among the paving, while on

one side of the garden are exquisite old-fashioned roses and long beds of massed delphiniums, including some varieties that have been at Pitmuies for more than 70 years. A rambling-rose hedge separates the Rose Garden from the yellow and blue borders which lead back to the house.

Along the Trellis Walk, clematis and climbing roses contrast with blue Himalayan poppies, and ferns, hostas and bergenias flourish close to a row of Tibetan cherry trees. Pinks and violas brighten the paved area and, in raised beds, there is a collection of old and

modern cinquefoils. In the Alpine Meadow, which was once the drying ground for the 18th-century 'Gothick' wash-house, autumn mowing encourages a marvellous display of snowdrops and crocuses in spring.

By early summer shrub roses border the Terrace Walk which leads to the Turbie Burn. Between the burn and the Vinny Water, beeches and limes shade the walk, overlooked by an extraordinary turreted dovecote which bears the date 1643 and the Ogilvy and Guthrie arms. The Vinny Garden has some variegated hollies and a paperbark maple, while the walk down to the Black Loch takes you through woodland interplanted with rhododendrons and azaleas.

Left: Massed planting in the borders creates dazzling blocks of colour

Right: The Rose Garden with a pattern of circles. Some of the hundreds of delphiniums – some plants more than 70 years old – can be seen on the left

Below: Snowdrops by the ornate bridge over the burn

INVEREWE GARDEN

Swathes of herbaceous borders with drifts of magenta flowers merging into blue then orange; woodland walks with exuberant splashes of rhododendron colour; ponds, bog gardens and leafy glades; a walled garden with an improbable mix of cottage-garden plants and exotic bulbs – all this and more now delights visitors to these gardens that perch on a rocky peninsula above the shores of Loch Ewe.

Inverewe Garden is the result of the rugged determination of one man, Osgood Hanbury Mackenzie, to overcome both probability and practicality. When Osgood, the younger son of Sir Francis Mackenzie, Laird

of Gairloch, and at the time only 20 years old, acquired the 12,000-acre (4,856ha) site in 1862 it was barren moorland and rocky coast. Fierce, salt-laden gales blew in from the Atlantic, burning and shrivelling any tender leafy plants in their path.

A century and a half later, Inverewe is now considered to be one of the most spectacular gardens in Scotland. It hosts a national collection of olearias, one of the most comprehensive collections of acid-loving rhododendrons in the United Kingdom (most notably the scarlet, winter-flowering *Rhododendron barbatum* with its dramatic wine-red trunks) and a significant

collection of ourisias – one variety of which is named 'Loch Ewe'. From spring to autumn and even in winter, the garden has both colour and interest.

In spring, snowdrops and snowflakes, dwarf daffodils, crocus and Californian dog's-tooth violets bloom along path edges and throughout the dappled woodland. In May and June the blended fragrances of *Choisya ternata*, Mexican orange blossom, deciduous yellow azaleas and the honey scent of the Madeiran spurge drift across the garden.

By summer, in the Walled Garden, the herbaceous borders dazzle with a mingling of flowers, herbs and vegetables. Clematis and

Left: Height is important in a garden on this scale

Right: Rhododendrons bloom in the woodland

Below: Ornate Victorian cloches nestle among the leeks
and dahlia seedlings

climbing roses clamber over pergolas and a
row of *Rosa* 'Silver Jubilee' underplanted with
lavender-coloured nepeta makes a beautiful
central feature.

In autumn, banks of predominantly blue
and purple hydrangea create a cloud-like
effect, scarlet maples enflame many a
vista, and the Tasmanian climber *Billardiera
longiflora*, its greenish-yellow flowers long
past, hangs with deep blue-purple fruits.
Then in winter there is colour on a grand
scale with the red blossoms of frost-hardy
Rhododendron 'Nobleanum'.

Whilst still building his Victorian mansion,
facing south towards the Torridon mountains

and his favoured stalking grounds, Osgood set about improving the impoverished soil by adding a mixture of peat, seaweed, manure and clippings and, folk memory has it, loam brought by boat from Ireland. Ever since, in this area with an average annual rainfall of around 78 inches (2 metres), tons of mulch are needed each year to replace the leached soil and continue to nurture the plants.

High walls of the local pink-coloured sandstone were built to shelter Osgood's first venture, a south-facing, 1-acre (0.4-ha) walled garden constructed on a former glacial raised beach. Conceived on almost cottage-garden lines, yet with plants from around the globe, this area has scarcely changed today. Huge decorative cabbages and aromatic herbs grow in harmony with delphinium and geraniums, Chatham Island (New Zealand) giant forget-me-nots and American cannas. A profusion of red hot pokers, blue Himalayan poppies, iris and agapanthus, purple allium, orange crocosmia and day lilies and tall, feathery bronze fennel compose a thrilling palette.

A further luxuriant herbaceous border runs along the front of the current Inverewe House – the original mansion having been burnt down in 1914. Osgood's daughter Mairi, who inherited both his passion for gardening and his estate when he died in 1922, created a courtyard garden in the ruins. Closer still to the shore, and often lapped by the tide, there is a rock garden which experiences the full force of salty storms.

In an area with a latitude of 50°, more northerly than Moscow and only 600 miles (965km) from the Arctic Circle, a substantial windbreak was essential. Osgood planted over 100 acres (40.5ha) of mainly salt-tolerant Scots and Corsican pines with, further inland, copses of alder, beech, birch and oak. It took over 20 years to establish the tree canopy. Only then could clearings be cut to create dense clusters of brilliant colour. Osgood loved the large-leaved rhododendrons newly introduced from China and the Himalayas. Some specimens of his 19th-century planting still flourish, notably *Rhododendron hodgsonii*, which reaches a height of 30 feet (10 metres) and bears rose-magenta flowers

through April and early May. Next to a rare rhododendron from Sri Lanka, in the area curiously named Bamboosalem, Osgood dedicated the only inscribed stone in the garden to the peace at the end of World War I.

From the outset, Osgood realised the importance of height in a garden on this scale and, in holes hewn out of the bedrock, he planted Tasmanian and Australian eucalyptus, now reputed to be some of the largest-growing trees in the world. Rare and tender palms were carefully sited for the drama of their silhouettes and giant gunnera edged the Bog Garden, contributing their own dramatic outlines.

Once thought to have been planted by Osgood's daughter Mairi in honour of US servicemen stationed in the area during World War II, an area called 'America' is now known to have been planted by Osgood in 1898 as a home for a range of American plants. Its crowning glory is a massive turkey oak (*Quercus cerris*), which might now have reached its potential height of 100 feet (30 metres). Other plants in this most sunny and sheltered area include alpine rhododendrons, Japanese and other maples, and South American bromeliads.

Over a period of 90 years with, it must be said, a little assistance from the warm currents of the North Atlantic Drift, father and daughter created a magnificent showplace that defied the elements. In 1952, a year before her death, Mrs Mairi Sawyer handed over the garden and part of the estate to the National Trust for Scotland to ensure that it would continue, as the founders had done, to welcome and delight visitors all year round.

INDEX

ACKNOWLEDGEMENTS

The Automobile Association wishes to thank the following photographers and organisations for their assistance in the preparation of this book. Abbreviations for the picture credits are as follows – (t) top; (b) bottom; (l) left; (r) right; (c) centre; (AA) AA World Travel Library

2-3 Clive Boursnell/Garden Picture Library/www.photolibrary.com; 6 MMGI/Marianne Majerus; 7 Christopher Miles/Alamy; 9 Derek St Romaine Garden Photo Library; 10 AA/Neil Ray; 11bl Mike Werkmeister/East Lambrook Manor Gardens; 11cr AA/David Hall; 11br AA/Richard Ireland; 12 Barnsley House; 13t Barnsley House; 13b Mark Bolton Photography; 14 Charles Hawes; 15bl Charles Hawes; 15r Charles Hawes; 16 Anna Stowe Botanica/Alamy; 17t Andrew Lawson/The Garden Collection; 17b Anna Stowe Botanica/Alamy; 18 NTPL/Stephen Robson; 19 NTPL/Stephen Robson; 20 Mike Werkmeister/East Lambrook Manor Gardens; 21l Mike Werkmeister/East Lambrook Manor Gardens; 21tr Mike Werkmeister/East Lambrook Manor Gardens; 21br Mike Werkmeister/East Lambrook Manor Gardens; 22 Mike Werkmeister/East Lambrook Manor Gardens; 23l Mike Werkmeister/East Lambrook Manor Gardens; 23r Mike Werkmeister/East Lambrook Manor Gardens; 24 Alice Kennard; 25 Heather Edwards; 26 MMGI/Marianne Majerus; 27 Andrew Lawson/The Garden Collection; 28 www.timgoodephotography.co.uk; 29 www.timgoodephotography.co.uk; 30 Claire Reid; 31 MMGI/Marianne Majerus; 32 NTPL/Paul Harris; 33 NTPL/Nick Daly; 34 Steve Taylor ARPS/Alamy; 35 AA/Richard Ireland; 36 MMGI/Marianne Majerus; 37 MMGI/Marianne Majerus; 38 MMGI/Marianne Majerus; 39t MMGI/Marianne Majerus; 39b MMGI/Marianne Majerus; 40l AA/David Hall; 40r AA/David Hall; 41 AA/David Hall; 42 NTPL/Paul Harris; 43t NTPL/Paul Mogford; 43b NTPL/Stephen Robson; 44 Julian Stephens/Heligan Gardens Ltd; 45 Heligan Gardens Ltd; 46bl NTPL/Mike Williams; 46br NTPL/David Dixon; 47 NTPL/David Dixon; 48 Elizabeth Bullivant; 49 Elizabeth Bullivant; 50t Elizabeth Bullivant; 50b Elizabeth Bullivant; 51 Daphne Hannam; 52 NTPL/Nick Meers; 53 NTPL/Neil Campbell-Sharp; 54 Derek Harris/The Garden Collection; 55 MMGI/Marianne Majerus; 56 Peter Barritt/Alamy; 57l Mike Greenslade/Alamy; 57r Stephen bond/Alamy; 58 Val Corbett/Country Life Picture Library; 59 Val Corbett/Country Life Picture Library; 60 AA/M Birkitt; 61l MMGI/Marianne Majerus; 61r Jonathan Buckley/The Garden Collection; 62 Weald and Downland Open Air Museum; 63 Weald and Downland Open Air Museum; 64 Pedro Silmon/The Garden Collection; 65 Susanna Bott; 66 MMGI/Marianne Majerus; 67t MMGI/Marianne Majerus; 67b MMGI/Marianne Majerus; 68 Derek St Romaine Garden Photo Library; 69 Derek St Romaine Garden Photo Library; 70t Derek St Romaine Garden Photo Library; 70b Derek St Romaine Garden Photo Library; 71 Derek St Romaine Garden Photo Library; 72 Broughton Castle, Oxon; 73t Andrew Lawson/The Garden Collection; 73b Andrew Lawson/The Garden Collection; 74 Derek Harris/The Garden Collection; 75 Derek Harris/The Garden Collection; 76 Nigel Quérée; 77l Nigel Quérée; 77r Nigel Quérée; 78 Linda Kennedy/Alamy; 79 Andrew Lawson/The Garden Collection; 80 MMGI/Marianne Majerus; 81t MMGI/Marianne Majerus; 81b MMGI/Marianne Majerus; 82 Jonathan Buckley/The Garden Collection; 83l Jonathan Buckley/The Garden Collection; 83r AA/John Miller; 84t Derek St Romaine Garden Photo Library; 84b Derek St Romaine Garden Photo Library; 85 Derek St Romaine Garden Photo Library; 86 Derek St Romaine Garden Photo Library; 87 Derek St Romaine Garden Photo Library; 88 www.harpurgardenlibrary.com; 89 AA/M Birkitt; 90 Derek St Romaine Garden Photo Library; 91 Derek St Romaine Garden Photo Library; 92 Fleur Robertson; 93 Loseley Park; 94 MMGI/Marianne Majerus; 95 MMGI/Marianne Majerus; 96 Richard Longfield; 97 Richard Longfield; 98l Mille Fleurs; 98r Mille Fleurs; 99 Mille Fleurs; 100 Penshurst Place & Gardens; 101 MMGI/Marianne Majerus; 102 Clive Nichols Garden Photography; 103t Clive Nichols Garden Photography; 103b Clive Nichols Garden Photography; 104 Arcaid Images/Alamy; 105 Clive Nichols Garden Photography; 106 Richard Raworth; 107 Richard Raworth; 108 Andrew Lawson/MMGI; 109 Charles Cottrell-Dormer; 110l Charles Cottrell-Dormer; 110r Charles Cottrell-Dormer; 111 MMGI/Marianne Majerus; 112 NTPL/Jonathan Buckley; 113 NTPL/Jonathan Buckley; 114 Spinners Garden; 115 Spinners Garden; 116t Louisa Arbuthnott; 116b Hodnet Hall Gardens; 117l Louisa Arbuthnott; 117cr MMGI/Marianne Majerus; 117br Dyffryn Gardens; 118t NTPL/Stephen Robson; 118b NTPL/Arnhel de Serra; 119 NTPL/Ian Shaw; 120 Charles Hawes; 121l Charles Hawes; 121r Charles Hawes; 122 Charles Hawes; 123 Adrian Sherratt/Alamy; 124 Dyffryn Gardens; 125t Dyffryn Gardens; 125b Dyffryn Gardens; 126 Charles Hawes; 127 Charles Hawes; 128 Hodnet Hall Gardens; 129 Hodnet Hall Gardens; 130 Arcaid Images/Alamy; 131b Arcaid Images/Alamy; 132 Louisa Arbuthnott; 133 Louisa Arbuthnott; 134 Charles Hawes; 135t Charles Hawes; 135b Charles Hawes; 136 MMGI/Marianne Majerus; 137 MMGI/Marianne Majerus; 138-139 MMGI/Marianne Majerus; 140 James Kerr; 141l Elton Hall; 141r AA/James A Tims; 142 Jerry Harpur; 143 Jerry Harpur; 144 Howard Rice; 145 Howard Rice; 146 MMGI/Marianne Majerus; 147 MMGI/Marianne Majerus; 148 Claire Birch; 149l Doddington Hall www.doddingtonhall.com; 149r Doddington Hall www.doddingtonhall.com; 150 MMGI/Marianne Majerus; 151 MMGI/Marianne Majerus; 152 MMGI/Marianne Majerus; 154 Elton Hall; 155l Elton Hall; 155r Elton Hall; 156 AA/Peter Baker; 157t John Hill/Alamy; 157b Hudson's Heritage/Haddon Hall; 158 Helmingham Hall; 159 Helmingham Hall; 160 Belinda Nelson; 161 Belinda Nelson; 162 www.monkie.co.uk; 163l www.monkie.co.uk; 163r MMGI/Marianne Majerus; 164 James Kerr; 165t James Kerr; 165b James Kerr; 166l MMGI/Marianne Majerus; 166r MMGI/Marianne Majerus; 167 MMGI/Marianne Majerus; 168 NTPL/Phil Evans; 169 NTPL/Phil Evans; 170 Clive Nichols Garden Pictures; 171 Clive Nichols Garden Pictures; 172 Dave Porter/Alamy; 173t Tracey Whitefoot/Alamy; 173b Christopher Miles/Alamy; 174 Clive Nichols Garden Photography; 175 Clive Nichols Garden Photography; 176 Derek St Romaine Garden Photo Library; 177 Derek St Romaine Garden Photo Library; 178t AA/John Morrison; 178b Dalemain; 179cl Arabella Lennox-Boyd; 179cr AA/Michael Moody; 179b Levens Hall & Gardens; 180 MMGI/Marianne Majerus; 181 Derek Harris/The Garden Collection; 182-183 English Heritage Photo Library; 183tr English Heritage/www.photolibrary.com; 184-185 Terry Foster/Alamy; 186 Dalemain; 187 Val Corbett/Country Life Picture Library; 188 Arabella Lennox-Boyd; 189 Arabella Lennox-Boyd; 190 MMGI/Andrew Lawson; 191 Jane Sebire/The Garden Collection; 192 Levens Hall & Gardens; 193 AA/E A Bowness; 194 Newby Hall; 195 Newby Hall; 196 Andrea Jones/Garden Picture Library/www.photolibrary.com; 197 John Glover//Garden Picture Library/www.photolibrary.com; 198 Clive Nichols Garden Photography; 199 Wildscape/Alamy; 200 Clive Nichols Garden Photography; 201 Clive Nichols Garden Photography; 202t Geoff Stephenson; 202b Pitmuies Garden; 203cl Ray Cox Photography; 203bl Geoff Stephenson; 203r Ray Cox Photography; 204 Geoff Stephenson; 205l Geoff Stephenson; 205r Geoff Stephenson; 206t Geoff Stephenson; 207 Ray Cox Photography; 208-209 Ray Cox Photography; 209tr Brian & Nina Chapple/National Trust for Scotland; 209br Brian & Nina Chapple/National Trust for Scotland; 210 Ray Cox Photography; 211 Brian & Nina Chapple/National Trust for Scotland; 212 Ray Cox Photography; 213t Brian & Nina Chapple/National Trust for Scotland; 213b Ray Cox Photography; 214 Pitmuies Garden; 215l Ray Cox Photography; 215r Ray Cox Photography; 216 Brian Chapple/National Trust for Scotland; 217l Ray Cox Photography; 217r Brian Chapple/National Trust for Scotland; 218 Brian Chapple/National Trust for Scotland; 219 Brian Chapple/National Trust for Scotland, endpapers AA/Karl Blackwell.

Every effort has been made to trace the copyright holders, and we apologise in advance for any unintentional omissions or errors. We would be pleased to apply any corrections in a following edition of this publication.